More SIMPLE QUILTS

with Splash, Dash & Panache

Nicole C. Chambers

TIGER LILY PRESS

To All My Friends —
Your generous hearts warm my soul

Acknowledgments

A heartfelt thank you to —

Vic and Lauren Clarke, affectionately known to some as "The Neighbors." The elegant ambiance of your beautiful Victorian home was a stupendous backdrop for these quilts.

Pat Chittenden, Michele Christiansen and Pat Lay, whose friendship I treasure. Thank you so very much for your seemingly limitless generosity and energy.

Ronda Beyer, for your quilting efforts that went well beyond the call of duty. Not only have I found a talented longarm quilter but a wonderful friend as well.

Jan Bechler, Elaine Braly, Marge Dennis, Diana Dunnington, Julie Kastl, Carol Ann Langstine & Berniece Skinner, for being the best "binding team" west of the Mississippi. How lucky I am to have such terrific friends.

Chris Murrell, for sharing your incredible talent and warm heart. Your inventiveness and savvy made these quilts really smile for the camera.

Francisco De La Moneda, for the many hours of diligent work you spent to insure the accuracy of these quilting instructions. It was my delight to have you as a partner in crime.

Aaron, for sharing your imagination and talent as well as your indefatigable sense of humor.

Editor: Aaron Chambers
Technical Editor: Francisco De La Moneda
Photography: Nick Garibbo
Photo Design
www.photo-design.com
Photo Stylist: Chris Murrell
Seams Sew Right Quilt Shoppe
www.seamssoright.net

The photographs in this book were taken at the beautifully restored Victorian home of the Clarke's
Italianate
built in 1884.
Portland, Oregon

Published by:

Tiger Lily Press
Portland, OR 97266
(503) 788-6772
tigerlilypress@msn.com
www.quiltmaniac.com
www.nicolechambers.com

Publisher's Cataloging-in-Publication Data

Chambers, Nicole C.
   More simple quilts with splash, dash & panache / Nicole C. Chambers. – 1st ed.
   p. cm.
   Includes index.
   LCCN: 2005900682
   ISBN: 0-9708375-0-X

   1. Patchwork quilts. 2. Patchwork–Patterns.
3. Color in textile crafts. I. Title.

TT835.C43 2005   746.46

Contents

Longarm Quilters Extraordinaire

Marilyn Badger
St. George, Utah

Marilyn has been producing award-winning quilts since 1991 including Best Longarm Quilt at the AQS Quilt Show & Contest at Paducah in 2004. She and her professional quilting techniques have been featured on over 50 PBS quilting shows with Fons and Porter and Kaye Wood, as well as Quilt Central with Donna Wilder and Janie Donaldson and HGTV's Simply Quilts with Alex Andersen. Marilyn's work has also been featured in national publications such as *Traditional Quiltworks, Sew Many Quilts, Love of Quilting, Quilter's Newsletter Magazine, Australia's Quilts Down Under, Great American Quilts 2004* as well as books by Nicole Chambers, Margaret Miller, Kaye Wood, Jennifer Priestley, Joyce Drexler, Karen Combs and Marion Haslam.

Having taught longarm classes for 11 years in her studio as well as in various parts of the United States, Canada, Australia and Japan, she is now retired from teaching and serves as a consultant to APQS. She is an active participant on their behalf at major quilt shows throughout the United States and Japan. ∎

Ronda Beyer
Little Gert's Creative Quilting
Tualatin, Oregon (503) 612-8502

Ronda's love of quilting started when she was very young, although one could surmise she inherited the quilting gene. Her mom, owner of Jane's Fabric Patch, and her Grandma Gert were both influential quilters in her life. They enthusiastically supported Ronda's early efforts which quickly bloomed into a full fledged love of quilting. Fond memories of quilting at her grandmother's knee inspired Ronda to name her longarm quilting business in her honor. Ronda believes that each quilt has its own personality and it is her responsibility to expand on that artistry. It is her commitment to enhance the quilt in a unique and individual way. To reach that end she believes communication is a key success factor.

Having been a quilter for many years, Ronda has a practiced eye for what will work in synergy with the concept of the quilt as well as benefit the entire design. One of her trademarks is an allover feather design that adds personality, depth and texture to the quilt, but that is only the beginning of her quilting repertoire. Ronda's quilting creativity has the benefit of insight and experience as to how the design will affect the final vision and personality of the quilt. If the agreed upon quilting design starts looking as though it may not measure up to that standard, you can bet you'll get a phone call from her. ∎

sewing machine, which she found fascinating. Merline began her own journey as a quiltmaker for relaxation during a time of high stress, but soon discovered it had become a very central facet in her life.

A talented and skilled quilter, Merline enjoys working with her clients, designing the quilting to carry through the ideas that they have pieced together. Her designs help to define as well as enhance what the quiltmaker has begun with their choice of colors, prints and patterns. Her inspirations come from everywhere. Merline enjoys sharing tips and techniques in classes she teaches for longarm quilters. ■

John and June Macauley
QuiltMasters
Brownsville, Oregon (541) 466-5494

John and June approach quilting from both a technical and artistic standpoint, each contributing their special talents. John brings 35 years of computer engineering skills and June, a former high school math teacher and avid quilter, brings an in-depth understanding of what goes into this special art. Together they have designed more than a hundred unique quilting designs. John and June were the first couple in the Pacific Northwest to incorporate a computer assisted longarm quilting machine.

John and June are no strangers to working as a team. Before embarking on their quilting career, they spent nine years sailing their 38' sailboat round trip from Seattle to New Zealand. John finds the programming, maintenance, and computer assisted quilting both interesting and challenging, while June enjoys working with their customers on a creative level, helping to incorporate their ideas into new designs and fine-tuning concepts for custom freestyle quilting. ■

Merline McLaughlin
The Cotton Yard
Eugene, Oregon (541) 689-5128

Quilts have been a part of Merline's life as far back as she can recall; her family brought quilts across the country in covered wagons during their migration in the 1850's. As a child, Merline can remember her paternal grandmother making quilt tops on her treadle

Pat Roche
Just Quilting
Portland, Oregon (503) 287-7266

Pat quilts in her home studio in Portland, where she lives with her husband Tom and daughter Sarah, bulldog Gracie and cat Ethel. Pat made her first quilt in 1976 and has never stopped quilting. The focus of her working life is machine quilting. Having bought her first longarm machine in 1998, she has devoted her time to mastering the art of longarm quilting by taking continuing education classes and running a very busy quilting business. Her goal is to make every quilt she quilts the best it can be. This care shows in the lovely quilts she produces as well as her loyal customer base. Pat has won numerous awards for her quilting. ■

Personalize Your Home with Your Works of Art

Have you ever wondered what that elusive combination of ingredients is that turn a house into a home, a home with style? What are those visual spices that reflect your unique sense of panache? What magic element exuberates warmth and welcome while still lending a visual excitement that makes you smile each time you enter the room? Certainly you have been in beautifully decorated rooms, lusciously colored and painstakingly furnished that still lacked a certain spark, while other rooms perhaps more humbly assembled sparkled with warmth and personality. This kind of home is more than just well chosen decorator colors hot off the pages of the latest magazines, more than architecture, and even more than stylish furniture and accessories. These rooms seem to have a will of their own, pulling you in and giving you that wonderful "glad you came" hug. They make you want to curl up on the sofa *(even if it's not your sofa)* and stay awhile.

Rooms, and in turn houses, radiate with a life force of their own. As a quilter, you quite literally have a magic wand that can turn any ordinary room into a space vibrating with energy, color, and best of all, love. What better way to express your unique creativity and still indulge your not-so-secret love affair with fabric? Let your home showplace your individuality. Let it be your private art gallery by simply filling it with color and texture … in other words, quilts.

My career in quilt design began with my pattern company *Nicole's Art to Live With.* From the very beginning my intention has been to bring you quilt designs that are visually exciting and add a touchable art to your life, art that could easily live in concert with your busy lifestyle, quilts that add style and visual drama but at the same time do not take a lifetime to make. Quilts that no matter where or how you decided to display them will not cause you to faint or get you sent to the big house for assault when someone happens to touch them with chocolate covered hands. The quilts in this book are indeed simple to make … yes, even the ones that don't look it. No matter which quilt you decide to make first, rest assured that you won't have to invest every spare moment of your life making it. The idea is to have fun sewing many, many quilts for your home. Believe it or not, most of the quilts shown in this book can be made in a weekend, unless you quilt the way a certain friend of mine does. Then it will take you a day.

Look around your home. Could you add a dash of color, a feeling of warmth or a smidgen of pizzazz? Maybe you want your room to look a touch more elegant, or perhaps you are feeling a bit whimsical. The right quilt will carry a big design wallop,

while at the same time be your most elementary design aspect. You can transform the look of a whole room by simply changing a few quilts. If your curiosity has been peaked, take a look at the quilts in this book. They have all been photographed in the same Victorian home. Hard to believe

isn't it? Each room has its own distinct personality.

If your home could use a bit of panache, fire-up the imagination and visualize some exciting colors that might add warmth to your rooms. Go ahead – take a few color risks. Quilts give you much

decorating freedom. They truly don't have to be a match to the decor to make your room look great. The colors simply need to fit into a general decorating scheme. Use this opportunity to open up and try things you've never dared. If the idea seems daunting to you, know that

everyone struggles a little at first. Trust that your instincts will guide you. If your color combination is comfortable to the eye, consider it a success no matter what the classic rules of decorating have to say. Use your newfound freedom to start creating an ambiance that reflects the real you.

Do you love animal prints but live with a very traditional decor? Indulge yourself. Art has its own rules. Who would have known when the great American poet Walt Whitman wrote: "Do I contradict myself/ very well then," he could have been talking about adding a leopard print to a traditional floral. There is always a way to subtly incorporate any fabric or color impulse into a design scheme. Show your pluck and let your house reflect the warmth and playfulness of your personality.

Use quilts to make your home glow with your unique creativity. Use quilts on chairs, sofas, and tables. Let your imagination roam free. Don't let old habits relegate your quilting talents to the bedroom. Sometimes large quilts are overlooked as wall hangings, a sizzling way to add color and personality to any room. If you came to visit me you would see it's one of my favorite ways to display my work – thus giving credibility to the old joke that quilters live in padded rooms. No, not because we're crazy, well, at least not in that straight jacket kind of way; we have simply discovered how to become decorator quick-change artists who can completely transform the look of a room in the few minutes it takes to change the quilts. So display your quilts as the works of art they are. Just a warning – you may not be able to get some people to leave the inviting ambiance. Be sure you check the sofa for any lingering guests before putting out the cat. ■

Creating Quilts with Lots of Personality

Have you ever wondered what separates a great quilt from a merely attractive one? Why some shake the room alive and others wilt like wallflowers? How can we be sure we are choosing fabric combinations that will make our quilts sparkle rather than languish? With the multitude of fabric choices that are available today, this is no easy task my friend, especially if your modus operandi involves picking fabrics willie nillie.

Quilts are more like people than you realize. Some make you laugh, some engage you, some you avoid, others you love, and others send you looking for another dose of caffeine. These differences are all a matter of personality — that intangible quality which defines the people we meet. The secret ingredient in the recipe for a quilt that makes you stand up and take notice is a dash of the unexpected, something a little different but not so much so that it throws the quilt out of kilter. A common problem among many quilts is that their fabrics are too closely matched. It's a little bit like going to a dinner party and finding all the guests have the same personality. What makes this an easy pitfall is the fact that it seems reasonable to match colors and styles. It feels as though we're stacking the deck in our favor to insure success but ironically it often does just the opposite, giving our quilts that homogenized look. Wouldn't you prefer showing up to a dinner party and finding a vast array of interesting people, rather than feeling like you're with a roomful of guests just like your mother-in-law? Of course choosing fabrics without connections to each other is not an improvement either since it will make your quilt look disjointed.

So what can we do to insure our quilts have oodles of pizzazz and personality? An obvious place to begin is with a focus fabric. Indeed this is a great beginning. But before you rush ahead, stop to consider what you want the total ambiance of your quilt to be. What that means is if you are making a floral quilt for your Aunt Sue because she loves flowers, don't stop there. You need more information in order to make good fabric choices. You will be miles ahead of the game if you take a few moments to consider the personality type of the floral quilt you are planning. You'll find that the choices for your supporting fabrics will start to come into focus and therefore be much easier to make. For instance, do you want your floral quilt's theme to be bold and dashing such as the theme fabric in *Bamboo,* giving the quilt a rich sultry tropical look? Or do you want something cool and elegant such as the floral used in *Lilacs & Lace?* Perhaps Aunt Sue would like something sophisticated, maybe with a traditional flair such as the theme fabric used in *Simple & Divine.* On the other hand, *Oooh La La's* theme fabric has a cosmopolitan feel to it. Notice that using the support

fabrics of black and white dots and stripes in combination with pink gives it a decidedly French look, n'cest pas?

The secret is to start with a central idea for your quilt and then focus on the concept or personality behind it. Already we've seen that a floral can have many varieties such as tropical, traditional, elegant, cosmopolitan and French. With this sort of direction, it is much easier to choose supporting fabrics. Don't forget, combining fabrics that are too similar will take the life out of a quilt so be sure to add a few zingers.

To get a better understanding let us examine the fabrics used in *Wild Wild West* and explore what makes them work well together. Since the theme fabric is a western print, the bandana fabric was an obvious choice as a significant support fabric. Upon closer inspection you may notice that although the black and tan fabrics are fairly nondescript

the red floral actually looks Victorian. It is this red, however, that gives this quilt its zip. Even though it is quite different from the other fabrics, it still feels at home on the ranch. Also, notice that the red and blue support fabrics do not "match" the reds and blues of the theme fabric. It is these two brighter support fabrics that give this quilt extra snap.

You don't always have to depend on a theme fabric to set the stage for a plucky personality. In these cases your quilt concept is like the scaffolding that holds up a building under construction. Let us take a look at *Mikado* and *Sail Away.* Although both quilts are made from the same pattern, they look strikingly different. While *Mikado* takes its strong Asian feel from the theme fabric, *Sail Away* has a nautical personality without having any theme fabric to speak of. The color combination of blue, white, yellow and red recalls clear water and yachting caps, but these same colors combined in a different way would yield a completely different result. It is the blue and white stripes combined with the large proportion of deep blue fabric that gives this quilt its unmistakable nautical look.

While in *Cherry Extravaganza* the theme fabric clearly dominates the quilt, its accents of clear yellow and red give it a bright and edgy personality. *Fruit Salad,* on the other hand, started out with a theme fabric that had a strong vintage reproduction look. Adding the crisp yellow and white stripes along with a vivid purple, orange and lime green gave this quilt a contemporary edge rather than the bygone era feel the theme fabric originally suggested.

It is truly amazing how many different personalities one quilt pattern can take on. It all depends on the combination of fabrics you put together. Give all of your quilts lots of personality and pizzazz by paying special attention to the choices you make while choosing both the theme and supporting fabrics. And always remember to add a little element of the unexpected. It gives quilts their own voices, and you'll love the way your quilts will start to sparkle. ■

Discovering New Fabric Dimensions

With so many gorgeous and easy-to-use fabrics available, it isn't any wonder that some distinctly strong graphic prints get pushed to the wayside. It's unfortunate that many quilters think of these fabrics as problematic and therefore decide to pass them by. The distinct direction and strong graphical nature of these prints can add an exciting dimension to your quilt that you can't create with color alone. It is true that these directional fabrics can be a little more thought provoking to use, but don't be tempted to let that dissuade you. It is precisely their strong directional nature that adds the extra oomph to many quilts. When preoccupied with putting a collection of fabrics together, it is easy to overlook the additional design dynamics a print has to offer. Make your quilts exceptional … the easy way. Take every opportunity to add these graphical treasures to your quilts. Even adding a graphical element as mundane as a stripe here or there will give a certain joie de vivre to your quilt. When you see a quilt you love, take a moment to examine the fabrics the quilter used. In many instances, it is the combination of these graphical elements of the print in concert with an interesting use of color that makes for a smashing quilt.

If using directional fabrics is a new experience for you, start out by adding these fabrics in small amounts. As with anything, it is best not to use too much until you become familiar and comfortable with using these types of fabrics. As a rule of thumb, don't let the proportion of strong angular fabrics overpower the others. Using them in smaller proportions will keep the other fabrics from looking like wimps in their presence. Of course there are exceptions to every rule, but this is a good starting place, at least until you feel comfortable trusting your own sense of design.

Diagonally printed fabrics can add a fabulous sense of drama to your quilt; and best of all, with almost no extra effort on your part. These fabrics offer so many unique possibilities that they should be in a class all to themselves. Their strong diagonal lines will give your quilt a feeling of energy and motion almost instantly. What a simple way to add movement and action. But don't relegate these fabrics solely to the supporting role. You can change the whole look of this fabric by simply cutting it into squares and then sewing the squares together to form a chevron. Voila! You have a custom theme fabric and a whole new look for your quilt. As you can see, the design premise of *Wild Thing* is based on exactly that idea. Try at least one diagonal fabric using this design technique. When you see how much fun it is to create your own chevron effects in this manner, you may find yourself looking at diagonals a whole new way.

Aside from obvious directional fabrics, another fabric style which slips under the radar of many quilters is angular allover prints. Because these fabrics tend to look overpowering they are easily overlooked, but don't be too quick on the draw to send them to the ugly duckling pile. After a careful look at what they have to offer, you may discover them to be hidden gems. Believe it or not, you can create stellar quilts by fussy cutting certain sections out of these "busy" fabrics. Many people use fussy cutting exclusively with fabrics which have a clearly separated motif, but this technique is a wonderful design tool for all types of fabric so make sure you keep it in your bag of tricks.

Begin by looking at these allover prints in small sections. Since it can be challenging to differentiate what part of the motif would look best within your design, make yourself a quick and easy viewing tool. It will make it easy to look at the different elements of the print one section at a time. From a sheet of paper, cut out a window the same size as the finished fabric square you will need. Then use the window to evaluate different parts of the print. Mark your fabric lightly in the corners of the square and then be sure to add $^{1}/_{4}$" seam allowance. Use a ruler and rotary cutter to cut out the squares. These fabrics will yield exciting and unusual effects if you just take the time to appreciate what they have to offer. ∎

Accent Fabrics that Give Your Quilt Style

If I had a donut for every quilter who seemed surprised at seeing my choices of accent fabrics used in my quilts … I'd have a lot of donuts. The beauty of accent fabrics is that you can find fun colors and textures without having to commit yourself to a whole quilt. What an excellent opportunity to add a little bit of sass to your quilt! The secret is to think outside of your normal comfort zone and indulge your unique sense of whimsy and flair.

A successful accent is both similar and different to the other fabrics used in the quilt. I know, easier said than done. Deciding on an accent that will add both style and panache can be confusing, but it doesn't need to be.

When choosing an accent fabric for your quilt, it is good to start with the goal of finding a fabric that relates to the general theme of the quilt, but not so much that it is visually absorbed by the other fabrics. Instead, it is more like an exclamation mark at the end of a sentence. You want to make a statement that sends a little zing to the viewer, enough to at least spark a second look. Perhaps you wouldn't think so but animal prints, a personal favorite of mine, make particularly fun accents. You may be tempted to think that because animal prints look so distinct on the bolt, they are too big of a risk for many quilts. After all, how can you insure that they will be a good fit with your fabric combination? Let us take a look at *Animal Magnetism* and see if we can find some answers. This leopard print is a good, risk-free choice for several reasons. For one, it continues the overall jungle theme of the main fabric. Also, the coloration of this print fits the colors of the theme fabric, actually too much to be the only accent. This brings us to another important reason. The leopard accent is a perfect support and companion for the main accent fabric which is the purple. The leopard's compatibility with the jungle inspired theme fabric makes it a fun beginning choice and adds a little kick to the overall fabric combination, but it could not have carried the quilt design without the additional purple accent. The purple, which is lighter and brighter than any of the purples represented in the theme print adds that spark and pizzazz the quilt needs while the leopard adds texture in an unexpected and fun way. A dynamic duo, the two accents working in unison; one brings the viewers attention and the other gives a little dash of panache.

Many times you can create a bit of fun and vivacity by simply introducing one accent color and letting it carry the whole responsibility. In *My Secret Garden* you may have noticed that using a brighter and livelier purple did the trick. The placement of that accent fabric, however, plays an important role in its perception. Surrounded by rich burgundy squares, the combination creates an exciting contrast. Again, notice that although the purple is not a surprising choice for an accent since purple is part of the main fabric's color scheme, it is much lighter and brighter. While contemplating how to use accent fabrics within your quilt, be sure to experiment with placement. An accent's placement has almost as much influence on the overall look as the color and texture of the fabric you choose.

You can really educate your artist's eye by noting how accent fabrics are utilized by other quilters. Find a quilt you admire and evaluate how and why that quilt's accents work. It will pay off in the long run. Let's use *Wild Thing* as our example and analyze how and why the red accent works. It's easy to see that the theme fabric is black and white, and the supporting fabrics are green, black and brown, but there is not a drop of red in any of these fabrics. Why then did it make a successful accent?

Since the accent squares are small, perhaps it is hard to discern that the red is an ethnic print. This is significant only because even though the color does not support the overall theme of the quilt, the print melds well with the black and white animal fabric. Even so, in large quantities the red would look out of kilter. In small doses, however, it adds a visual excitement that doesn't disrupt the overall design. When putting these fabrics together, I simply followed my taste and instinct, much like you do. On the other hand, I didn't choose this fabric at random either. To give you something to hang your hat on, let's uncover the underlying design logic and discover why the red makes a great accent fabric.

First, the fabric's ethnic personality made it a possible contender for this quilt design … but red? Why did that seem like a good addition to this particular fabric combination? Have you noticed how every December we are visually reinforced that red and green make a great color combination? And perhaps you recall the discussion of the color wheel in my 1ˢᵗ book, *The Quilt Maniac's PLAYBOOK*. If so, you probably remember that red and green are complimentary colors. This means they just about come with a written guarantee of compatibility. Placing the red next to the brown print helps bring down the intensity of this vivid red accent. Why did the brown bring down the red's brightness? Again, if you remember the color wheel, brown is a shade of orange and therefore a close relative of red. This information is relevant because it tells us that red and brown are compatible since they are color wheel neighbors. That color similarity works to dilute the intensity of the red because the brown, a cousin of red, provides a soft contrast, whereas placed next to green, the contrast would have been heightened as well as giving the quilt a "holiday" look.

Finding interesting and fun accents can be confusing at first. You want the fabric to both "fit" and "be different" all at the same time. It is a good idea to examine how other quilts incorporate accents and what exactly makes them work, or not work, as the case may be. See if you can trace back the ideology of how and why that color or texture is a successful combination, much as we did for *Wild Thing*. It will be time well spent. Having a knack for using accents well is a real power tool in your quilting repertoire. ■

So Many Fabrics ...
So Many Choices

Ask any quilter what they love best about quilting and they will most likely tell you it's choosing the fabrics. Ask any quilter what gives them the biggest pain in the-you-know-what and they will probably tell you it's choosing the fabrics. Obviously quilters both struggle and rejoice with this aspect of quilting. Part of the problem is that when faced with the challenge of choosing fabrics from amongst all the color and print combinations, the possibilities are quite literally endless. Change one fabric and your quilt can take on a whole new personality. Move your fabric to a different part of the quilt and again you have a completely different look. If choosing the perfect fabrics for your quilt has made you want to reach for a straight jacket on occasion, be comforted to know that you have lots of company.

To keep from becoming overwhelmed by the plethora of fabrics available today, it is often a good idea to develop a strategy for how to go about choosing fabrics. Believe it or not, the order in which you choose your fabrics can turn a daunting task into one that is simple and downright fun. Strategies help because from the very onset you can narrow the field of possibilities, while at the same time work towards developing the look and personality you desire.

When you are working on a two-color quilt such as *Ronda's Delight* or *Butterscotch Sundae*, the order in which you choose your fabrics is, of course, not an issue. With two-color quilts you need to focus your attention on how much contrast you want to create within that combination of fabrics.

It is important to realize that you don't necessarily need a great disparity between light and dark fabrics to get a successful effect. Many times the opposite is true. A stark black and white fabric combination can have an almost blinding contrast and give the quilt an edgy contemporary feel. On the other hand, using

a softer contrast such as the antique white toile in combination with black, like in *Ronda's Delight*, lets the eye make a smoother transition as it travels from one fabric to the other. This mellowed yet still dramatic combination creates a warmer, more inviting quilt. When you hear tan and white, it probably doesn't set your heart aflutter. You might think too mundane to be interesting but *Butterscotch Sundae* manages to hold its own. The golden tan batik is actually fairly light in value but when placed next to white, it is still strong enough to create a significant contrast. What is also helpful in this particular instance is that the main fabric does not have a print and the full color saturation of the batik gives this fabric great presence in the quilt. How light or dark a color appears to be is completely dependent on what

color you place next to it. This is an important fact to remember while looking for fabrics. As you consider your desired effect, keep an eye on the range of contrasts you are using. Although a strong contrast may look very pleasing while the fabric is still in one piece, fabrics can start to look harsh and edgy when they are cut up in smaller pieces. This is especially true in two-color quilts because they have no other colors to bridge the contrast gap. Toning down the contrast a notch or two will still give your quilt lots of color dimension, but will also move your color

combination into a more pleasing light to dark ratio.

Then again, what about the other end of the spectrum when you have a quilt that needs a gazillion fabrics? Finding the fabrics for some of these quilts at first glance can feel a bit intimidating. For these instances, approaching the fabric selection in a particular order is a good technique. For an example let's walk through the steps of choosing fabrics for *Lilacs & Lace* together. Since we will need ten *(yikes)* fabrics for this quilt, let's start by finding the two most important ones, namely the theme and background fabrics. It only makes sense to start with the theme fabric since it will give us an indication of what color families to consider for the quilt's color palette. The background fabric, in this case, is important because it is so visible and thus it becomes a dominant force in the design. Once we find these two fabrics, the hardest part is already done. We want

to choose the background fabric early in the game because it will significantly influence the other potential fabric choices. The supporting fabrics that will look appealing with our background will depend on whether the background is from the warm or cool color family, whether it is white or a color, and whether it is a print or a solid fabric. The white in *Lilacs & Lace* gives this quilt a cool elegant feel while it makes the colors within the theme fabric literally sparkle, rather than washing them out. You could have created a completely different quilt by making the background fabric light lavender, light green or possibly even gray. In this case, the stark white gives the soft supporting fabrics a crisp contrast that works particularly well and adds a touch of sophistication.

Once satisfied with the background and theme fabrics, we next need to choose the darkest fabric. Again, consult your theme and background fabrics to give you a color direction. Keep in mind that in this

instance as well we won't need to create a huge contrast between the dark and background fabrics to achieve a good result. At the same time we want to prevent making the contrast too soft, letting the fabrics mush together into an indefinable mass of color and pattern. A good rule of

thumb is to choose a dark fabric strong enough to hold the design from a distance of at least 6 feet. In other words, we want this part of the quilt to be easily defined and not melt into the background. It is usually difficult to gauge the balance of contrast at close range. It is easy to see each individual fabric at close range,

but many fabrics lose their individuality when viewed as a group or from a distance. Also, as you know, when fabrics are cut into small pieces they can look like distant cousins from the fabric on the bolt. When using prints always pay special attention to the light parts of the print and evaluate whether they have enough contrast with the background. With prints it is easy to create visual holes if the light areas don't have enough contrast with the background fabric.

Next, we will choose the medium-dark fabric. This fabric needs to be a lighter value than the dark fabric, but only enough to create a soft contrast. Now that we have decided on these four key fabrics, the quilt's parameters are set. Because the rest of the fabrics will include colors and patterns that compliment these original four fabrics, choosing them will be much easier. As we

evaluate the remaining fabrics, keep an eye out for value in relation to the other fabrics already chosen. Nor do we have to limit ourselves to only the colors represented in the theme fabric. Take artistic license and add one or two that are slightly different just for the fun of it. Another

good rule of thumb is to choose soft colors for the receded areas, stronger colors for areas that need attention or define the quilt design. If getting a good balance in your quilts is hard for you, find the soft support fabrics first before moving on to their stronger counterparts. These in-between areas of the

quilt need colors that won't steal the show but are still noticeable enough to hold the quilt design. In the instance of *Lilacs & Lace*, the gray cornerstones as well as the lavender connecting squares have enough color to highlight the design but most definitely take a back seat to the more prominent support colors. As you see, choosing the many fabrics for this quilt was actually a process of elimination. Once we have a group of fabrics that look like they will work well together, it will be much easier to tweak choices and experiment a little here and there.

Quilting never seems to lose its sense of newness and adventure because we get to play masters of illusion. The change a simple combination of colors

and prints has on a quilt design can seem almost magical. We can even conjure up a special look just by combining fabrics that hint at our theme. *Oooh La La* is a great example of that. Although none of the fabrics look particularly French, the combination of pink and black triggers the mind in that direction. By adding the stripes and polka dots the quilt starts exuding a certain joie de vivre. Since I have yet to find a

polka dot that I didn't love, this quilt was big fun to put together. Since stripes and dots work so well together, this was an easy duo to add to the black and pink mix. This quilt gets an extra-special zip from the black dots on white contrasted against white dots on a black background. It is important to note, however, that the black dots on the white background are placed randomly while the white dots on the black

background are geometrically spaced. If both fabrics had been printed identically the combination could have easily looked stilted. This small but significant difference in the print adds interest to the quilt. Matching pattern styles of fabrics too closely can be as lethal to a great quilt design as over matching colors. Always give yourself the design freedom to make each fabric different even if it is only in the most subtle way.

Sometimes that freedom manifests itself with using unusual color combinations. It can be fun to challenge ourselves to use certain colors. This was how the fabric combination in *Argyle* came to be. If you've read any of my previous books, you'll no doubt be familiar with my assertion that gray is one of the most underused and unappreciated colors. Gray can add a great color element. Plus, it can make many quilts look particularly masculine, which I suspect comes as a relief to many men. It can also give quilts an air of sophistication. What's important to keep in mind when using gray is that since it is such a neutral influence, particular attention needs to be paid to the other fabrics in the mix. *Argyle* needed fairly spunky colors not to be overwhelmed by the large amount of gray. The blue, purple and gold accents really brighten the color scheme while the gray background offers the perfect backdrop to show these colors to their best advantage. The black lends the quilt a little bit of drama, and is also the perfect way to create a vibrant contrast between the gold accent fabric, which by-the-way, is what actually makes this quilt sparkle.

Have you noticed that recently many gorgeous large-scale fabrics have made their way onto quilt shop shelves? It's almost impossible to resist them. Since often times large-scale prints turn into a completely different looking fabric when

cut into small pieces, they have not been extremely popular with many quilters in the past. *Bamboo* is a great way to show off these large-scale prints in all their splendor. Aside from showcasing a beautiful large-scale print you love, the important element in making this quilt design successful is choosing great accent fabrics. Keep in mind, however, that when working with large-scale fabrics there is a big temptation to match colors to the main print too closely. If you don't add a few zingers to balance out the theme fabric, it can become too dominant. Using an interesting balance of color, value and texture that both contrasts and coordinates with the theme fabric makes for a good fabric combination in these instances. In the case of *Bamboo*, the addition of the leopard print in orange and aubergine adds spice while the aubergine batik adds a richness to the overall color scheme. Surprisingly, the official accent fabrics turned out to be black and dark green. It just goes to prove that choosing effective accents does not necessarily mean choosing bright fabrics.

Toile is another under appreciated dandy that is too often admired and then put back on the shelf. Too many quilters consider this fabric problematic, and unfortunately it never finds its way into their quilts. This misconception is due to toile's strong presence; often it must be thought of as a theme and background fabric at the same time. In addition, since it has only two colors, many quilters find themselves stymied by what other fabrics might collaborate well with it. Add to that the fact that this type of print is usually large and directional; it is no wonder many quilters shy away from adding this beautiful fabric to their quilting repertoire. Although there are some elements that must be addressed in order to use toile successfully, it is by no means a difficult fabric.

Frenchie is a good example of what makes for a good combination when using toile as the focal point while still adding other colors into the mix. In this particular pattern the toile is comfortable being both the background and theme fabric, a very good start. Black makes a good support fabric for his print because it offers a dramatic contrast, giving the toile a depth and richness. Adding accents of blue, red and gold bring in just enough color to make the quilt interesting because they are somewhat unexpected but at the same time they do not steal the show from the black and white toile print. If the accent colors had been used in larger quantities, it is quite likely they would overwhelm the toile. As you see, in small ratios they add a special flair without interfering with the strong black and white theme of this quilt. The black and white stripes add just a little zip without complicating the color scheme.

A good rule of thumb when working with toile fabric is to think of the toile as filling the role of both the theme and background fabrics. However, don't feel you have to limit yourself to only their color scheme. Rather think in terms of adding a few accent colors in small amounts. Also, don't overlook the opportunity to add interest by introducing other fabric patterns in the same colors as the toile.

It is without question that the fabric makes the quilt. It is what makes quilting so much fun and interesting and yet it is also what tortures us. Many quilters think that because they struggle with this process they are somehow lacking in talent. This is simply not true. By experimenting and trying out new print and color combinations, we educate our eye to become better and better at creating interesting fabric combinations. Give yourself the freedom to not stay content practicing only the safe tried and true ideas, rather give your creativity a chance to shine, and to explore new ideas. It is by risking failure that we ultimately learn how to succeed. ■

A New Age in Quilting

As we look at the ocean of quilts that have been made through the years, we can readily see the evolution of our art, much like the rings on a tree. Each generation of quilters has produced a crop of work that reflects their unique life experiences as well as the materials of their time, thus turning each quilt into a microcosm of personal history. Sometimes we are lucky enough to know their stories and other times, as we study and appreciate their efforts, we can only speculate on who they were and what the story of their lives may have been. For those of us lucky enough to have a collection of these quilts, we can hold some of their history, known or unknown, in our hands and wonder who these women and men were and how they had accomplished these beautiful works of art.

It is often thought that in days gone by, when everyday chores involved much more physical labor than they do now, quilters primarily made quilts for utility, a way to recycle scraps of fabric into usable bed coverings for the family. Although I'm sure that many quilts were made for just this purpose, it is also amazing that the time and effort was taken to make these quilts beautiful. It's almost unimaginable to think that after having done backbreaking work during the day, they still had enough energy to follow their creative impulses. It does prove that ultimately our desire to express this creativity within us is a driving force behind every quilt we make. Even though our art form gives us the advantage of producing practical as well as decorative end results, in the end it is this creative force that entices us to make more and more quilts. How else can you explain that unbridled enthusiasm you feel when you find a fabric that just makes your heart sing. If you are like me, you can hardly wait to get into your sewing room to try it out, just to see how it will look.

And as many quilters will admit with some chagrin, it also explains the UFOs that we all have tucked away in our closets.

Although I can remember my quilting experiences before the advent of some of the tools that we now take for granted, it is hard to imagine myself quilting without the benefit of the multitude of rulers, choice of seam rippers and dear God … please don't take my rotary cutter away from me. We all have our collection of favorite tools that make easy work of most quilting projects. In contrast, it is truly amazing to realize that the artistry that the quilters of bygone years produced were made without any of these luxuries.

But just as we appreciate the contributions of the quilters who have come before us, one does have to wonder what the generations that follow us will have to say about the collection of quilts we leave behind. As we luxuriate in the vast choices of fabric and tools at our disposal, how will our quilts speak of our creativity, our view of life, long after we are gone? It is perhaps ironic that even though our lives are much easier in comparison to those a hundred years ago, they are at the same time also that much more complicated. What we have gained in convenience, it seems we have lost in time and yet quilters are producing more quilts than ever before.

Walk though any quilt show and you could easily surmise that our quilting legacy can easily be summed up by the freedom and variety by which we use color and technique to achieve our creative visions. Our bounty of materials has manifested itself into a wide assortment of quilting styles. We are the first generation of quilters who have been blessed with an almost unlimited pool of color and textures to draw from, which can be readily seen in the quilts we produce today. Color is a huge focus of our quilting efforts, just look at the rich color combinations of the quilts everywhere around you. What do you suppose quilt historians will say as they examine these works of art? Will they be surprised at our fabric combinations as we leave these bits of ourselves for posterity? Will they be able to date our quilts simply by the amount of turquoise or orange they contain? It makes one almost laugh with anticipation as we ponder their reactions and at the same time we may find ourselves wondering what their quilts will look like.

So as we continue the tradition of quilting, it is the natural order that we add new aspects to our art. This is highly evident in the techniques we use in making quilts today. From the most humble nine-patch quilt to the impressive art quilts you see hanging in museums and private collections, you can see how we've used our ingenuity to unleash our special creativity. New technology has lead to new techniques. We have even managed to turn office equipment into quilting tools. And still it is quite certain that we have only scratched the surface of what is possible. Perhaps the best lesson we can pass on to future quilters, however, is the same one that they have passed on to us. To take what is available and then find new ways to interpret the possibilities they offer our quilts. ■

Quilt Gallery

Midnight Sun

Approximate size: 74" x 74"
Made by: Nicole Chambers
Quilted by: Marilyn Badger

If you are looking for a quilt that is big on design and easy to make, *Midnight Sun* is the one for you! You will be amazed at how ultra simple this quilt really is. Believe it or not, if you know how to make a nine-patch, flying geese and half square triangles, this quilt is in the bag. Instructions are on page 123.

Sail Away

Approximate size: 71" x 71"
Made by: Nicole Chambers
Quilted by: Merline McLaughlin

As you can see from the two other versions of this quilt design, this fast and easy quilt can lend itself to many different looks. It is a great way to show off theme fabric plus most quilters can make this quilt in a day ... no kidding! Instructions are on page 107.

Mikado

Approximate size: 71" x 71"
Made by: Nicole Chambers
Quilted by: Ronda Beyer

If you look at *Sail Away* and *Animal Magnetism* you'll see the completely different quilt personalities you can create by simply changing the fabrics. It's a fun way to use those favorite fabrics you can't bear to cut up. Instructions are on page 107.

Butterscotch Sundae

Approximate size: 70" x 70"
Made by: Pat Chittenden
Quilted by: Ronda Beyer

There is a special charm that is unique to two-color quilts, not to mention that choosing the fabrics for them is a real cinch. This little gem will go together quicker than a wink. Make your quilt elegant, full of fun or go for big drama. Instructions are on page 79.

Argyle

Approximate size: 64" x 64"
Made by: Michele Christiansen
Quilted by: Ronda Beyer

It's my theory that there are many men who secretly stress over the idea that they'll end up with a "feminine" quilt. Actually I've overheard many interesting conversations on this subject while shopping for fabric. Although this quilt can take on many personalities depending on the fabrics you choose, this particular combination will make many men smile. Instructions are on page 102.

Simple & Divine

Approximate size: 84" x 105"
Made by: Pat Lay
Quilted by: Ronda Beyer

You may be tempted to ask ... how can any feathered star be simple? Believe it or not, to make this feathered star you use no set-in seams at all, only half square triangles. Instructions are on page 91.

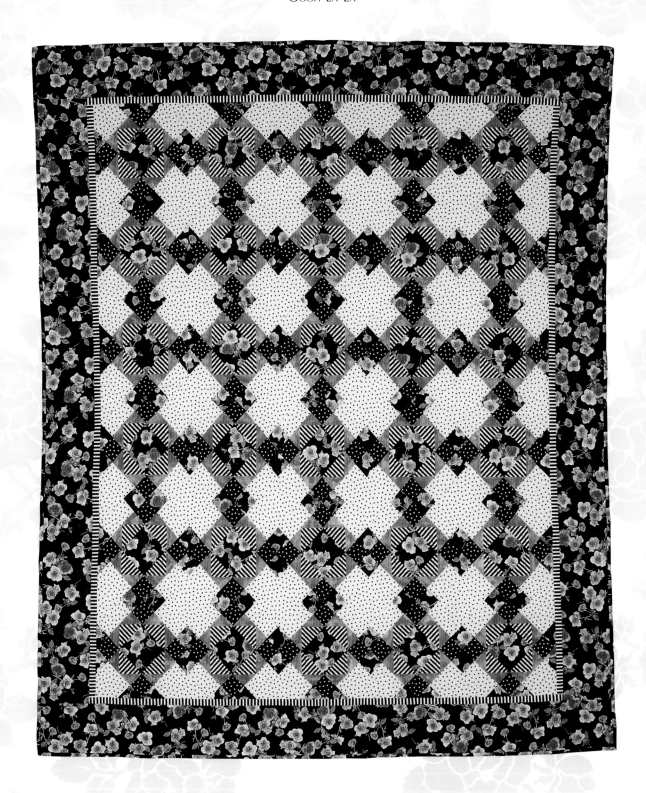

Oooh La La

Approximate size: 70" x 81"
Made by: Nicole Chambers
Quilted by: Ronda Beyer

It must be confessed ... I indulged myself unabashedly and used polka dots and stripes to my hearts content. This fun quilt is made from two simple blocks that are set on point. But don't let my dot mania influence you too much. This design lends itself well to using many fabrics so put on your thinking cap and turn to page 135 for the instruction.

Fruit Salad

Approximate size: 52" x 64"
Made by: Nicole Chambers
Quilted by: Merline McLaughlin

Do you ever get in the mood to make a quilt that is truly a no brainer but at the same time won't bore you into a comatose state? This quilt is just the ticket when you want to sew something that is ultra simple. So get out that fabric you've just been itching to sew, add a few zingers for spice and really get things dancing in your sewing room. Instructions are on page 112.

Animal Magnetism

Approximate size: 71" x 71"
Made by: Pat Chittenden
Quilted by: Merline McLaughlin

Are you an animal print lover like me and sometimes find yourself wondering how to use them without ... well, looking like you were a biker chick in your last life? Combine them with a theme fabric that suggests flora and fauna and you're on your way. This is an ultra easy quilt to make so feel free to experiment ... the lucky recipient may just be happy enough to purr. Instructions are on page 107.

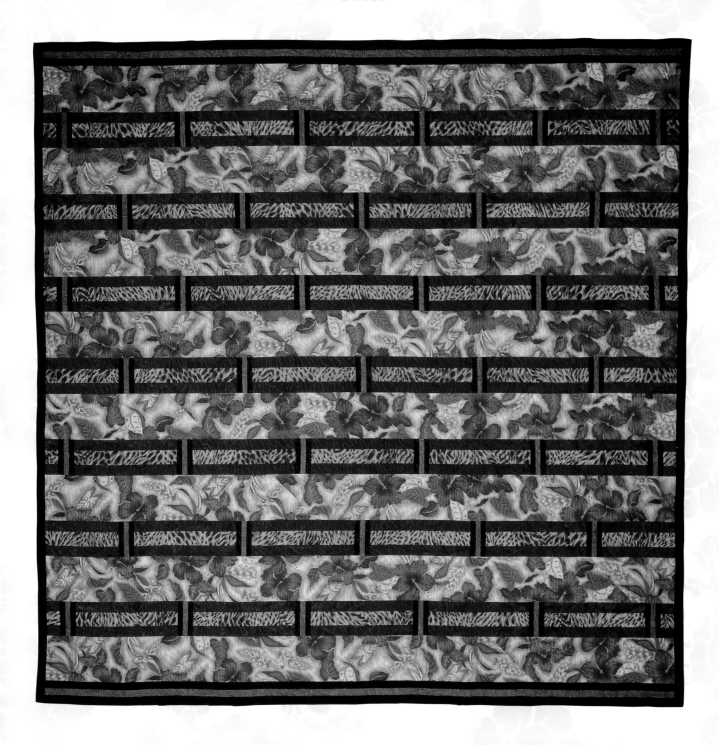

Bamboo

Approximate size: 94" x 96"
Made by: Nicole Chambers
Quilted by: June & John Macauley

Have you been admiring those fabulous large-scale prints and wondering what you could do with them? Ponder no more my friend, this super-easy quilt is a great way to showcase those fabrics. The simple lines of this design is an easy way to give your bedroom style. Instructions are on page 64.

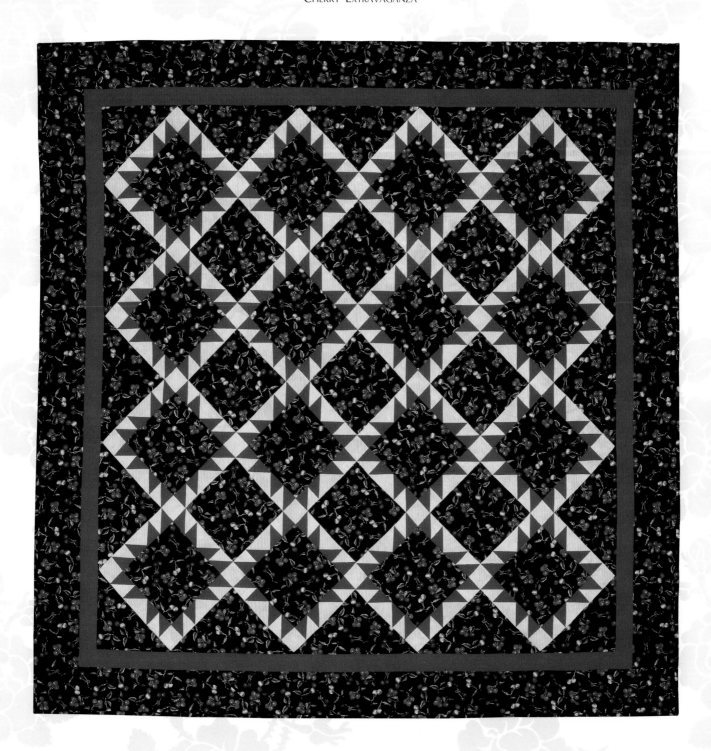

Cherry Extravaganza
Approximate size: 73" x 73"
Made by: Pat Chittenden
Quilted by: Ronda Beyer

This is the quilt to make when you L-O-V-E the theme fabric and absolutely hate the idea of having to cut it up. All you'll need to add are two accent fabrics for an extra little kick and this quilt is on it's way to being done! Instructions are on page 74.

Fitzwilliam & Ross

Approximate size: 75" x 88"
Made by: Nicole Chambers
Quilted by: Merline McLaughlin

This quilt pattern will surprise you. It is a surprisingly simple quilt to make. Give your quilt a look of yesteryear or make it totally trendy. This quilt design will look great in a wide variety of fabrics. Instructions are on page 96.

My Secret Garden

Approximate size: 71" x 71""
Made by: Michele Christiansen
Quilted by: Ronda Beyer

Have you forgotten someone's birthday and need to make a quilt in a really big hurry ... like a day? When a sewing blitz is on your horizon, this quilt design does not sacrifice style for speed. Simply find a theme fabric that makes you smile, add a couple of accent fabrics and Voila! Instructions are on page 86.

Amsterdam Windmills

Approximate size: 74" x 74"
Made by: Pat Chittenden
Quilted by: Ronda Beyer

The perfect quilt for a pinwheel maven ... whether you love making them or know someone who loves just looking at them. This quilt consists of simple-to-make blocks that fit together to form the two different pinwheels. Looks can be deceiving, this quilt is made entirely of squares and rectangles. Instructions are on page 130.

Ronda's Delight

Approximate size: 70" x 70"
Made by: Ronda Beyer
Quilted by: Ronda Beyer

When my friend Ronda quilted *Butterscotch Sundae* she fell in love with the quilt. In my cunning and devious attempt to coax her into giving me back the quilt, I offered her the pattern. Being a good friend, she offered to make another version of this design. She finished this quilt so fast, it almost gave me whiplash. "I love, love, love this quilt pattern," she said, "and you can quote me on that," and as you see, I have. Instructions are on page 79.

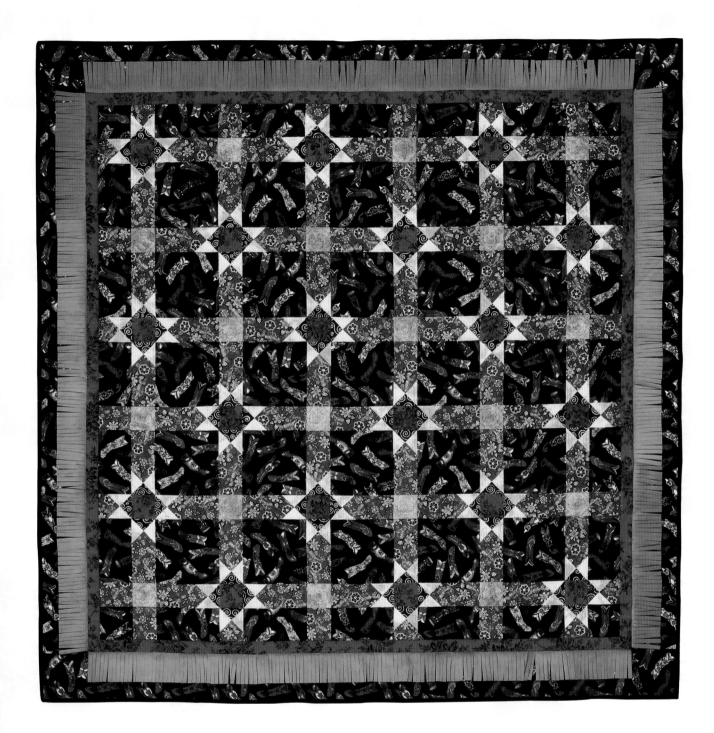

Wild Wild West

Approximate size: 70" x 70"
Made by: Nicole Chambers
Quilted by: Pat Roche

Indulge your whimsey with this design and give your cowpoke the quilt of his dreams. What fun it is to pull together a western theme and then add the fringe just for a little bit of extra pizzazz. So put on your boots, find your favorite western print and mosey on over to your sewing machine, partner. Quicker than the shake of a horses tail, this quilt will be in your saddlebag. Instructions are on page 68.

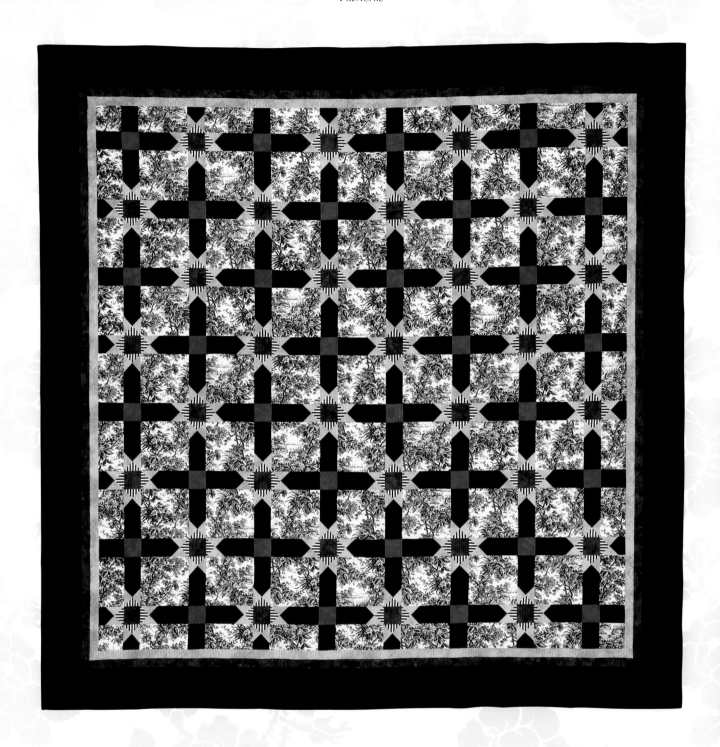

Frenchie

Approximate size: 90" x 90"
Made by: Pat Lay
Quilted by: Ronda Beyer

With this quilt pattern in your bag of quilting tricks, you will be able to make even the most persnickety fabric prints sit down and behave themselves. It offers a particularly successful way to show off directional theme fabrics such as toile while still giving you a place to add accents for a bit of dash and panache, plus it is a slam dunk to make. Instructions are on page 68.

Lilacs & Lace

Approximate size: 73" x 73"
Made by: Nicole Chambers
Quilted by: Ronda Beyer

Ok ... I'll fess up ... this quilt will give you a workout on the cutting table ... but after that it is a very simple quilt to make. A little bit of paperpiecing in the main block gives this quilt much design milage while the other parts and pieces of the blocks are simple and basic. Instructions are on page 116.

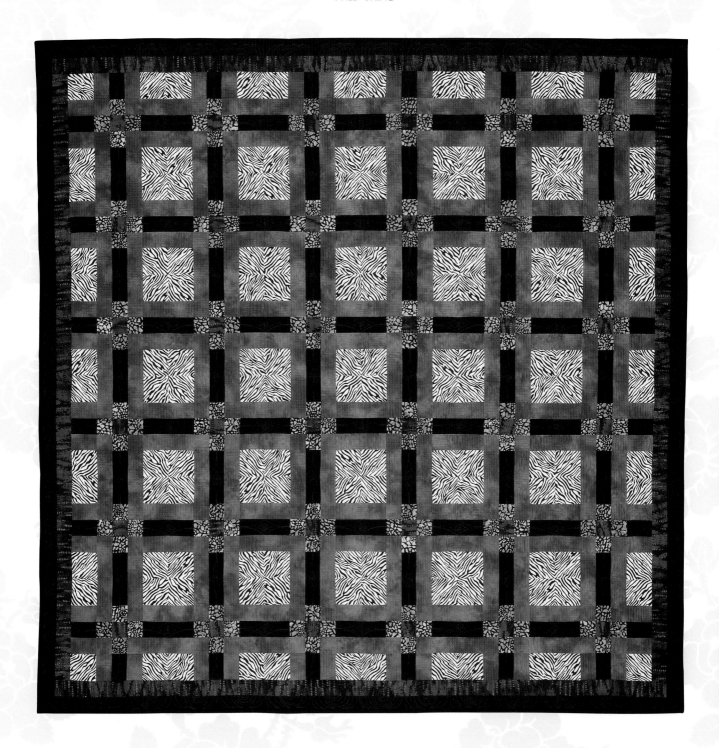

Wild Thing

Approximate size: 63" x 63"
Made by: Nicole Chambers
Quilted by: Ronda Beyer

Have you wondered what fun effects you could create with diagonally printed fabrics? The central block of this quilt is actually 4 squares sewn together. It's amazing how many effects you can create, not to mention it is fun ... fun ... fun. Instructions are on page 86.

Italian Tile

Approximate size: 52" x 64"
Made by: Pat Chittenden
Quilted by: Merline McLaughlin

Even the most simple shapes can create a pretty snazzy quilt when you use an interesting combination of fabrics. Give yourself the freedom to experiment a little. Fussy cut fabrics you normally wouldn't think of as candidates and watch your quilt start to sparkle. Instructions are on page 112.

Hog Heaven

Approximate size: 75" x 88"
Made by: Pat Chittenden &
Nicole Chambers
Quilted by: Ronda Beyer

Do you have a motorcycle enthusiast in your life? Or perhaps your sweetie has other hobbies he loves. This easy quilt design offers many options to show off novelty fabrics to their best advantage. Instructions on page 96.

Step-by-Step
Instructions

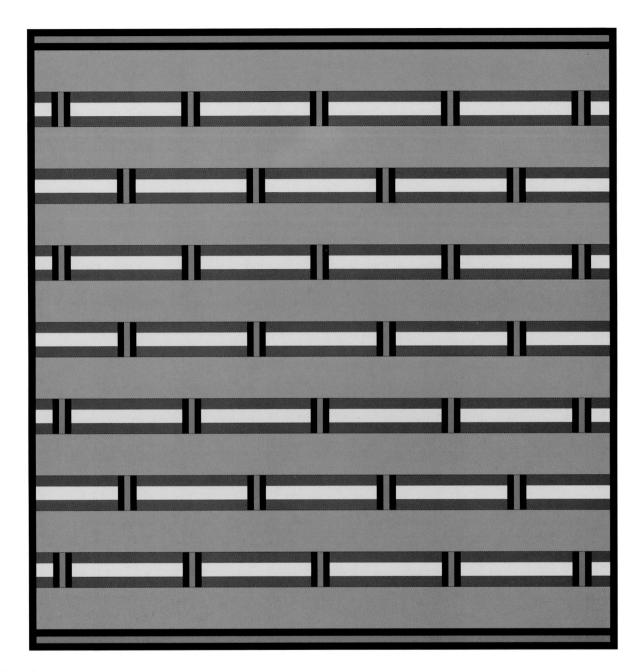

Bamboo *approximate size 94" x 96"*

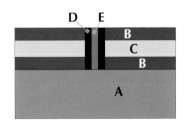

Fabric Requirements: *color photos are on pages 32 and 51*

Fabric A	$4^2/3$* yards
Fabric B	$2^1/4$
Fabric C	$1^1/2$
Fabric D	2*
Fabric E	$^5/8$

Includes binding

Cutting Instructions for Bamboo

NOTE: *These cutting instructions are based on having 40" of usable fabric width. If your fabric is even slightly wider, you may have strips left over.*

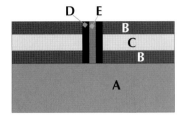

Fabric A

21 strips	7" wide

Fabric B

36 strips	2" wide

Fabric C

18 strips	2¹/₂" wide

Fabric D

12 strips	1¹/₄" wide
Border	
15 strips	1¹/₂" wide
Binding	
10 strips	2¹/₂"

Fabric E

6 strips	1¹/₄" wide
Border	
5 strips	1¹/₂" wide

Sewing Instructions

With right sides together, sew fabric C 2¹/₂" and fabric B 2" strips together lengthwise as illustrated in Figure 1. Make 18 strip sets. Press seams as arrows indicate. Cut pieced B/C strip sets into 15¹/₂", 11¹/₄" and 2¹/₂" sections, as indicated.

Figure 1

Make 18 strip sets and cut into sections as indicated

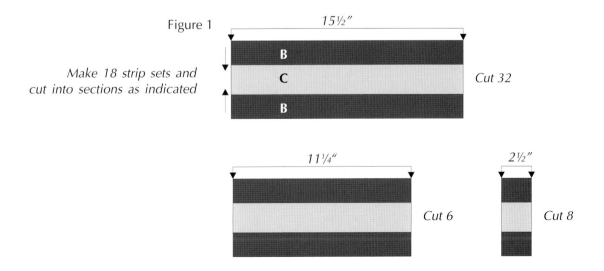

With right sides together, sew fabric D and E 1¹/₄" strips together lengthwise as illustrated in Figure 2. Press seams as arrows indicate. Cut pieced D/E strip sets into 5¹/₂" sections.

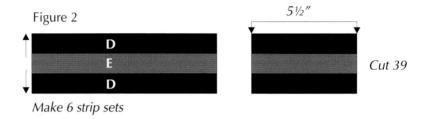

Figure 2

5½"

D
E
D

Cut 39

Make 6 strip sets

Sew D/E sections and B/C sections together to form rows A and B as illustrated in Figure 3. Press seams as arrows indicate.

Figure 3

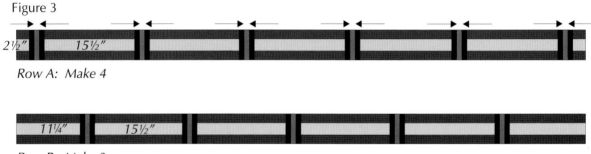

2½"   15½"

Row A: Make 4

11¼"   15½"

Row B: Make 3

Measure the length of the rows you have just pieced. Be sure to measure rows A and B through the centers. Use diagonal seams to piece 8 fabric A 7" strips to the measured length of the rows. Press seams open.

Designer Tip: *If the length of the rows are slightly different, compute the average length and piece all fabric A strips to that one length.*

Refer to Figure 4. Sew 2 fabric A strips onto each side of row A. Press seams as arrows indicate.

Figure 4

A

A

Make 4

Sew row B between pieced rows A as illustrated in Figure 5. Press seams as arrows indicate.

Figure 5

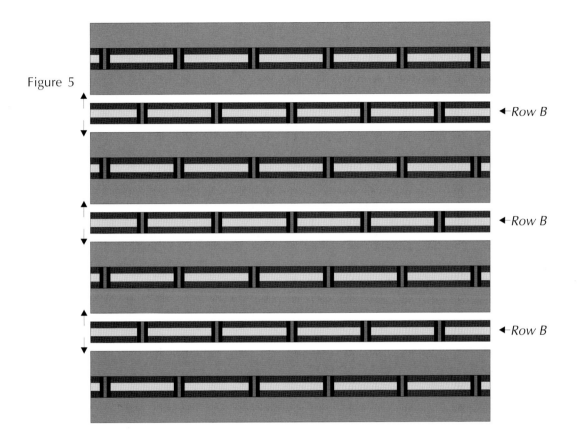

←Row B

←Row B

←Row B

Border

Begin by making 3 long strips of fabric D (1½") and 1 long strip of fabric E (1½"). Each of these long strips consist of 5 fabric strips sewn end to end with a diagonal seam. Cut these long strips in half. *(Each strip will measure approximately 100" long depending on the width of your fabric.)*

Sew these half strips into strip sets as illustrated in Figure 6. Press seams as arrows indicate.

Figure 6

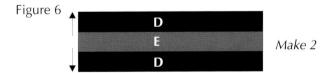

Make 2

Measure the *width* of your quilt *(through the center of the quilt)* and trim pieced strip sets to that measurement. Sew to top and bottom of the quilt and press seam towards outer edge. Measure the length of your quilt and trim the 2 remaining fabric D strips to that measurement. Sew to each side of the quilt and press seam towards outer edge.

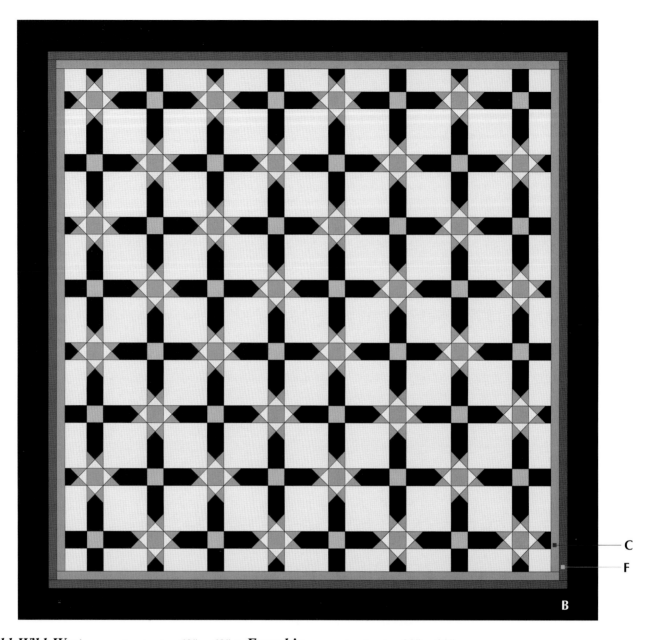

Wild Wild West *approximate size 68" x 68"* • **Frenchie** *approximate size 90" x 90"*

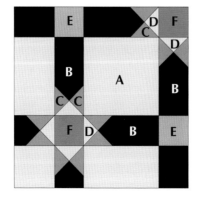

Fabric Requirements: *color photos are on page 14, 35, 57 and 58*

	Wild Wild West *(lap)*	**Frenchie** *(queen)*
Fabric A	$3^1/2$*	$3^1/4$* yards
Fabric B	$1^1/2$	$5^1/8$
Fabric C	$1^1/8$	$2^1/8$
Fabric D	$^1/2$	$^7/8$
Fabric E	$^1/4$	$^3/8$
Fabric F	$^3/4$	1
Ultra Suede **OR**	$^3/4$	—
Ready to use fringe	$7^1/2$	—

*Includes binding

NOTE: *These cutting instructions are based on having 40" of usable fabric width. If your fabric is even slightly wider, you may have strips left over.*

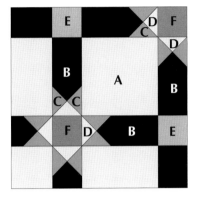

Cutting Instructions for Wild Wild West *(Lap size)*

Fabric A

5 strips	7¹/₄" wide	Cut into (25) 7¹/₄" squares
4 strips	4" wide	Cut into (20) 4" x 7¹/₄" rectangles
scraps		Cut into (4) 4" squares

Outer border

7 strips	5¹/₂" wide	

Binding

7 strips	2¹/₂" wide	

Fabric B

12 strips	3"	Cut into (60) 3" x 7¹/₄" rectangles
3 strips	3"	Cut into (24) 3" x 4" rectangles

Fabric C

6 strips	3" wide	Cut into (72) 3" squares
◣ 4 strips	3³/₈" wide	Cut into (36) 3³/₈" squares

Fabric D

◣ 4 strips	3³/₈" wide	Cut into (36) 3³/₈" squares

Fabric E

2 strips	3" wide	Cut into (18) 3" squares

Fabric F

2 strips	3" wide	Cut into (18) 3" squares

Inner border

6 strips	1³/₄" wide	

Ultra Suede *(fringe)*

6 strips	3¹/₄" wide	

◣ *Do NOT cut these strips if you plan on making half square triangles by drawing a grid or using products such as Triangle Paper™ or Triangles on a Roll™*

NOTE: *These cutting instructions are based on having 40" of usable fabric width. If your fabric is even slightly wider, you may have strips left over.*

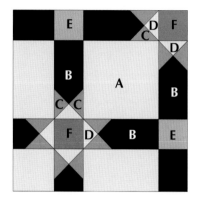

Cutting Instructions for Frenchie *(Queen size)*

Fabric A

10 strips	7¹/₄" wide	Cut into (49) 7¹/₄" squares

For directional fabrics, cut the 4" x 7¹/₄" rectangles in two orientations so that the print is in the correct direction when placed in the rows

3 strips	4" wide	Cut into (14) 4" x 7¹/₄" rectangles–*top/bottom rows*
2 strips	7¹/₄" wide	Cut into (14) 7¹/₄" x 4" rectangles–*at ends of remaining rows*
scraps		Cut into (4) 4" squares

Fabric B

23 strips	3" wide	Cut into (112) 3" x 7¹/₄" rectangles
4 strips	3" wide	Cut into (32) 3" x 4" rectangles

Outer border

10 strips	6" wide

Binding

10 strips	2¹/₂" wide

Fabric C

10 strips	3" wide	Cut into (128) 3" squares
◣ 6 strips	3³/₈" wide	Cut into (64) 3³/₈" squares

Inner border 1

9 strips	1³/₄" wide

Fabric D

◣ 6 strips	3³/₈" wide	Cut into (64) 3³/₈" squares

Fabric E

3 strips	3" wide	Cut into (32) 3" squares

Fabric F

3 strips	3" wide	Cut into (32) 3" squares

Inner border 2

9 strips	1³/₄" wide

◣ *Do NOT cut these strips if you plan on making half square triangles by drawing a grid or using products such as Triangle Paper™ or Triangles on a Roll™*

Sewing Instructions

Using a sharp pencil, draw a diagonal line on the wrong side of fabric C 3" squares. *(Using the Angler 2 or drawing a sewing guide onto your machine will eliminate this step.)*

Figure 1

Fabric C 3″ squares
Lap size: 72
Queen size: 128

Place fabric C 3" square onto fabric B 3" x 7$\frac{1}{4}$" rectangle as illustrated in Figure 2. Sew on the pencil line. Press seams as arrow indicates and then trim seam allowance to measure $\frac{1}{4}$". Repeat, using fabric B 3" x 4" rectangle and fabric C 3" square.

Figure 2

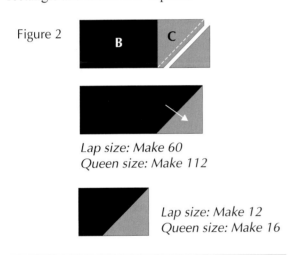

Lap size: Make 60
Queen size: Make 112

Lap size: Make 12
Queen size: Make 16

NOTE: *Be sure you have the following fabric B 3" x 4" rectangles left over:*
Lap size: 12 rectangles
Queen size: 16 rectangles

Place fabric C and D 3$\frac{3}{8}$" squares right sides together. Cut them in half diagonally. Sew triangles together on the wide edge. Press seam towards darker fabric and trim off dog ears.

Figure 3   3″

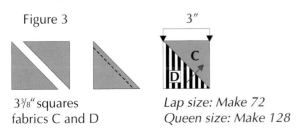

3$\frac{3}{8}$″ squares
fabrics C and D

Lap size: Make 72
Queen size: Make 128

Designer Tip: *If you are using stripes for fabric D, be sure to cut fabric D as illustrated. Notice that stripes are running vertically.*

Refer to Figure 4. Using a sharp pencil, draw a diagonal line on the wrong side of fabric C/D half square triangles.

Figure 4

Lap size: Mark 72
Queen size: Mark 128
3" half square triangles

With right sides together, position a half square triangle onto fabric B/C rectangles as illustrated in Figure 5. Use the same end where you previously sewed a fabric C 3" square *(Figure 2)*. **Sew on the pencil line in the direction indicated by the arrow in Figure 5.** Press seam and trim seam allowance to measure $\frac{1}{4}$".

Figure 5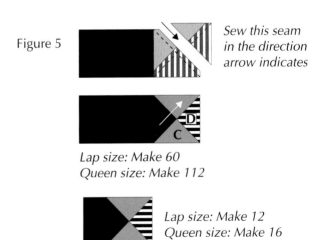

Sew this seam in the direction arrow indicates

Lap size: Make 60
Queen size: Make 112

Lap size: Make 12
Queen size: Make 16

Refer to Figure 6. Sew B/C/D units, fabrics A, B, E and F squares together to form indicated rows. Press as arrows indicate. For *Frenchie,* the arrows within fabric A squares and rectangles indicate fabric print direction.

Figure 6

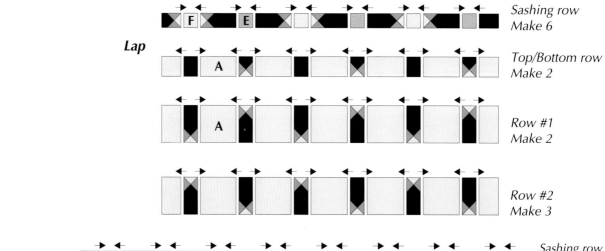

Sashing row
Make 6

Lap

Top/Bottom row
Make 2

Row #1
Make 2

Row #2
Make 3

Queen
*Directional
fabric*

Sashing row
Make 8

Top row
Make 1

Row #1
Make 4

Row #2
Make 3

Bottom row
Make 1

Sew rows together in the sequence illustrated in
Figure 7 and press.

Figure 7

Queen

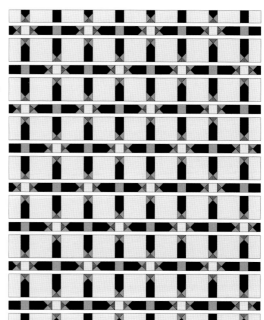

Lap

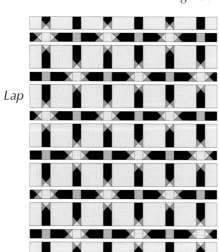

Borders

Frenchie

Measure the length of your quilt *(through the center of the quilt)* and piece 2 fabric C (1³/4") inner border 1 strips to that measurement. Sew to sides of quilt and press seam towards outer edge. Apply inner border 1 to the top and bottom of the quilt using the same technique.

Repeat these steps using fabric F (1³/4") inner border 2 strips.

Repeat these steps, this time using fabric B (6") outer border strips.

Wild Wild West

Inner Border

Measure the length of your quilt *(through the center of the quilt)* and piece 2 fabric F (1³/4") inner border strips to that measurement. Sew to each side of the quilt and press seam towards outer edge. Apply inner border F to top and bottom using the same technique.

Making Fringe

Use ready-made fringe or make your own using the following method. On the wrong side of the Ultra Suede (3¹/4") strips, draw a guide line ³/8" from outer edge along the length of strip. Then draw vertical lines ³/8" apart as illustrated in Figure 8. Carefully cut fabric along these vertical lines to make fringe. Do not cut past the guide line you drew across the width of the strip.

Figure 8

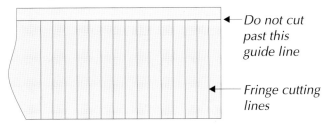

←— Do not cut past this guide line

←— Fringe cutting lines

Attaching Fringe and Outer Border

Measure the length of your quilt and piece 2 fabric A (5¹/2") outer border strips to that measurement.

Begin by aligning, right sides together, the uncut edge of fringe sections to the raw edge of inner border F. Next, pin sections to raw edge. Start ³/8" from one edge of inner border, butt sections, and finish ³/8" from the edge of the other inner border.

In order to sew fringe and outer border onto quilt simultaneously, pin outer border strips on top of already pinned fringe sections. Sew quilt, fringe and outer border layers together removing pins as you sew. Press seam towards inner border.

The steps to attach fringe and outer border to top and bottom of the quilt are similar to the above instructions. Measure width from edge to edge of outer border just attached. Piece 2 fabric A (5¹/2") outer border strips to that measurement.

As before, with right sides together, align uncut edge of fringe sections to raw edge of the inner border. Pin butted sections to raw edge. Make sure fringe sections meet at each corner. Sew fringe and outer border simultaneously by pinning outer border strips on top of already pinned fringe. Sew fringe and border to quilt, removing pins as you sew. Press seams towards inner border.

IMPORTANT NOTE: *Ultra Suede is easily damaged by excessive heat. Before pressing suede test on scraps to make sure iron is not too hot and use a pressing cloth.*

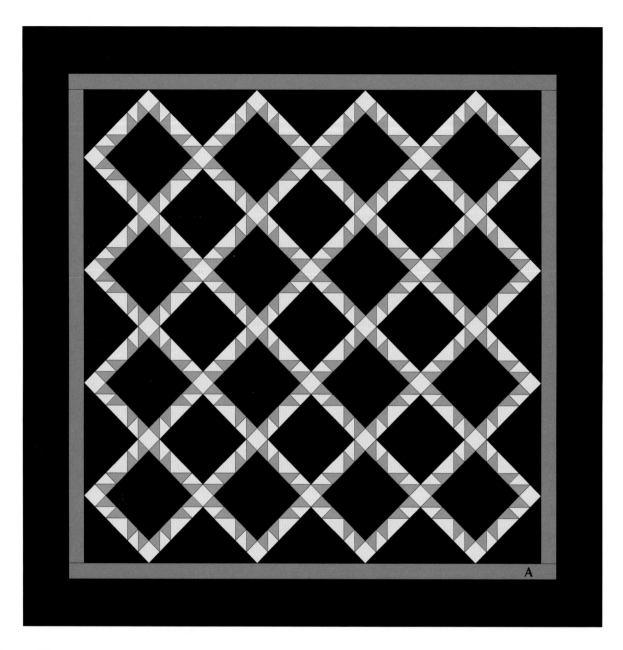

Cherry Extravaganza *approximate size 73" x 73"*

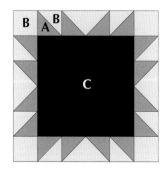

Fabric Requirements: *color photos are on pages 13 & 52*

Fabric A	$1^3/4$ yards
Fabric B	$1^1/2$
Fabric C	$4^1/2$*

*Includes binding

NOTE: *These cutting instructions are based on having 40" of usable fabric width. If your fabric is even slightly wider, you may have strips left over.*

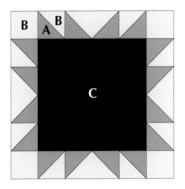

◤ *Do NOT cut these strips if you plan on making half square triangles by drawing a grid or using products such as Triangle Paper™ or Triangles on a Roll™*

Cutting Instructions for Cherry Extravaganza

Fabric A
8 strips	2¹/₂" wide	Cut into (128) 2¹/₂" squares
◤ 5 strips	2⁷/₈" wide	Cut into (64) 2⁷/₈" squares

Inner border
7 strips	2¹/₂" wide	

Fabric B
4 strips	4¹/₂" wide	Cut into (64) 4¹/₂" x 2¹/₂" rectangles
◤ 5 strips	2⁷/₈" wide	Cut into (64) 2⁷/₈" squares
3 strips	2¹/₂" wide	Cut into (40) 2¹/₂" squares

Fabric C
7 strips	8¹/₂" wide	Cut into (25) 8¹/₂" squares

Setting triangles
2 strips	15¹/₂" wide	Cut into (3) 15¹/₂" squares and *cut in half diagonally twice*

Corner triangles
scraps		Cut into (2) 9¹/₂" squares and *cut in half diagonally once*

Outer Border
7 strips	5¹/₂" wide	

Binding
7 strips	2¹/₂" wide	

Sewing Instructions

Draw a diagonal line on the wrong side of fabric A 2¹/₂" squares. *(Using the Angler 2 or drawing a sewing guide onto your machine will eliminate this step.)*

Figure 1

128 fabric A 2½" squares

With right sides together, position a fabric A 2½" square on one end of fabric B 4½" x 2½" rectangle as illustrated in Figure 2. Stitch on the pencil line. Press seam allowance towards outer edge and then trim to measure ¼". Repeat on the opposite end to complete A/B unit.

Figure 2　　　　　　　　　　　　　　　　Make 64

Use your favorite technique to make half square triangles or use the following method.

Place fabric A and B 2⅞" squares right sides together. Cut them in half diagonally. Sew triangles together on the wide edge. Press seam towards darker fabric and trim off dog ears.

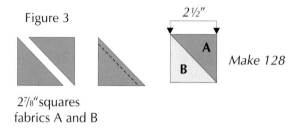

Figure 3

2½"

Make 128

2⅞" squares
fabrics A and B

Refer to Figure 4. Sew half square triangles and fabric A/B units together to make 64 Units 1. Sew fabric B 2½" squares to 20 of these units to make Unit 2. Press seams as arrows indicate.

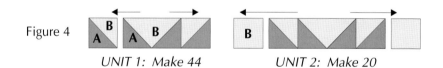

Figure 4

UNIT 1: Make 44　　　　　UNIT 2: Make 20

Sew Unit 1 to sides of fabric C 8½" square to form the block as illustrated in Figure 5. Press seams as arrows indicate.

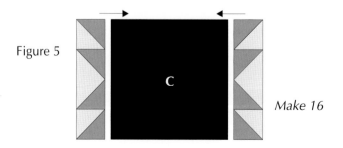

Figure 5

C

Make 16

Sew Units 1 and 2 in alternating order as illustrated in Figure 6. Notice that fabric A triangles in Units 1 are pointing up and in Units 2 are pointing down. Press seams as arrows indicate.

Figure 6

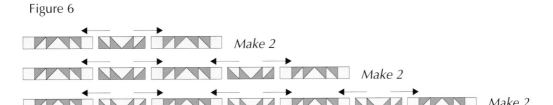

Sew blocks and fabric C 8¹/₂" squares in alternating order as illustrated in Figure 7 to form rows. Press seams as arrows indicate.

Figure 7

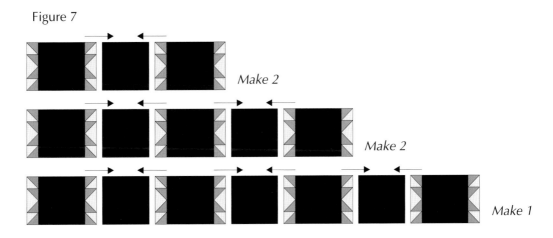

To complete rows, sew units *(Figures 4,5,6 and 7)* together as illustrated in Figure 8. Press seams as arrows indicate. Sew setting triangles to each end of rows and press.

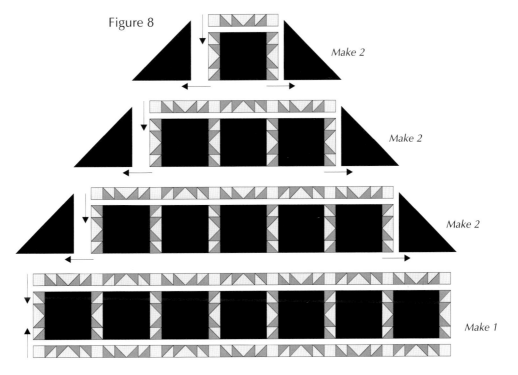

Refer to Figure 9. Sew rows together as illustrated. Press seams as arrows indicate. Sew corner triangles to quilt and press.

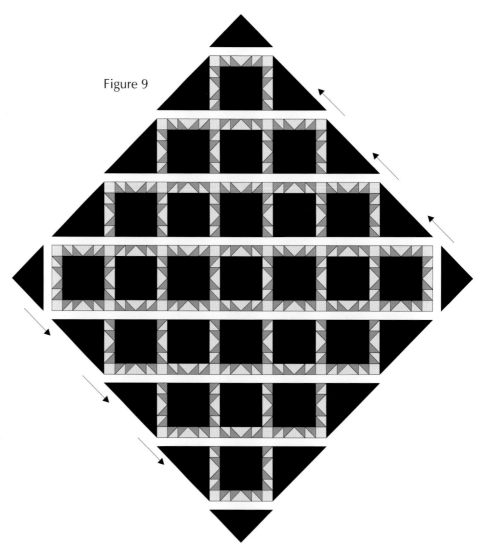

Figure 9

Border
Measure the length of the quilt *(through the center of your quilt)* and piece 2 fabric A (2^1/2") inner border strips to that measurement. Sew to each side of the quilt and press towards outer edge. Apply inner border to top and bottom of the quilt using the same technique. Repeat these steps this time using fabric C (5^1/2") strips for outer borders.

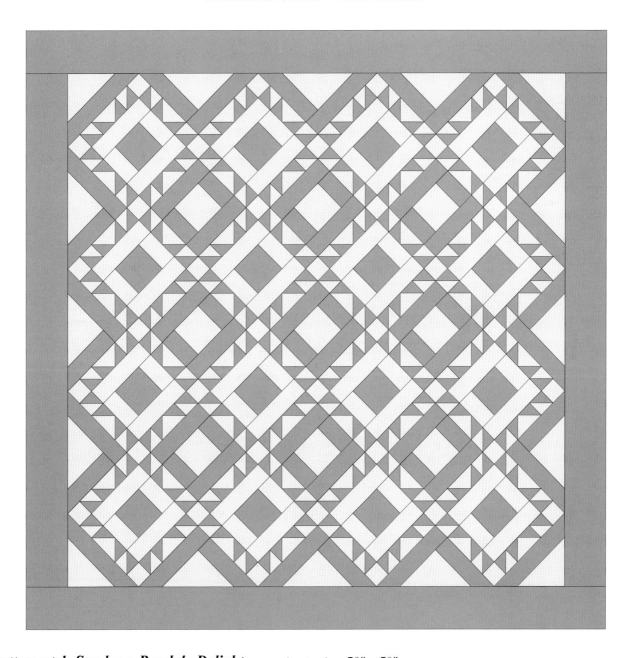

Butterscotch Sundae • Ronda's Delight *approximate size: 70" x 70"*

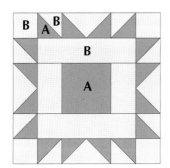

Fabric Requirements: *color photos are on pages 24, 30, 45 and 56*

Fabric A	$4^1/2$*
Fabric B	3

Includes binding

NOTE: *These cutting instructions are based on having 40" of usable fabric width. If your fabric is even slightly wider, you may have strips left over.*

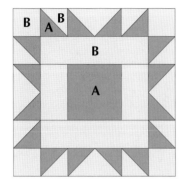

Cutting Instructions for Butterscotch Sundae • Ronda's Delight

Fabric A

2 strips	4^1/$_2$" wide	
8 strips	2^1/$_2$" wide	Leave 3 strips whole Cut into (18) 2^1/$_2$" x 8^1/$_2$" rectangles
8 strips	2^1/$_2$" wide	Cut into (128) 2^1/$_2$" squares
◣ 5 strips	2^7/$_8$" wide	Cut into (64) 2^7/$_8$" squares
7 strips	2^1/$_2$" wide	Cut into (12) 2^1/$_2$" 10" rectangles and (12) 2^1/$_2$" x 12" rectangles
2 strips	2^1/$_2$" wide	Cut into (4) 2^1/$_2$" x 14^1/$_2$" rectangles

Border
7 strips	5^1/$_2$" wide

Binding
7 strips	2^1/$_2$" wide

Fabric B

2 strips	4^1/$_2$" wide	
12 strips	2^1/$_2$" wide	Leave 4 strips whole Cut into (32) 2^1/$_2$" x 8^1/$_2$" rectangles
4 strips	4^1/$_2$" wide	Cut into (64) 4^1/$_2$" x 2^1/$_2$" rectangles
◣ 5 strips	2^7/$_8$" wide	Cut into (64) 2^7/$_8$" squares
3 strips	2^1/$_2$" wide	Cut into (40) 2^1/$_2$" squares

Setting triangles
1 strip	9^3/$_4$" wide	Cut into (3) 9^3/$_4$" squares and *cut in half diagonally twice*

Corner triangles
1 strip	6^1/$_2$" wide	Cut into (2) 6^1/$_2$" squares and *cut in half diagonally once*

◣ *Do NOT cut these strips if you plan on making half square triangles by drawing a grid or using products such as Triangle Paper™ or Triangles on a Roll™*

Sewing Instructions

Draw a diagonal line on the wrong side of fabric A 2$\frac{1}{2}$" squares. *(Using the Angler 2 or drawing a sewing guide onto your machine will eliminate this step.)*

Figure 1

128 fabric A 2½" squares

With right sides together, position a fabric A 2$\frac{1}{2}$" square on one end of fabric B 4$\frac{1}{2}$" x 2$\frac{1}{2}$" rectangle as illustrated in Figure 2. Stitch on the pencil line. Press seam allowance towards outer edge and then trim to measure $\frac{1}{4}$". Repeat on the opposite end to complete A/B unit.

Figure 2

Make 64

Use your favorite technique to make half square triangles or use the following method.

Place fabric A and B 2$\frac{7}{8}$" squares right sides together. Cut them in half diagonally. Sew triangles together on the wide edge. Press seam towards darker fabric and trim off dog ears.

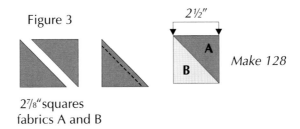

Figure 3

Make 128

2$\frac{7}{8}$" squares
fabrics A and B

Refer to Figure 4. Sew half square triangles and fabric A/B units together to make 64 Units 1. Sew fabric B 2$\frac{1}{2}$" squares to make 20 Units 2. Press seams as arrows indicate.

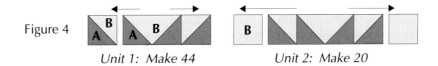

Figure 4

Unit 1: Make 44   *Unit 2: Make 20*

With right sides together, sew fabric B 2¹/₂" and fabric A 4¹/₂" strips together lengthwise as illustrated in Figure 5. Press seams as arrows indicate. Cut pieced strip into 4¹/₂" sections.

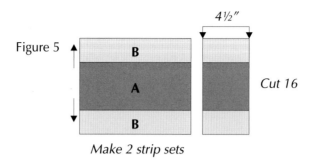

Make 2 strip sets

Repeat the last steps, this time using fabric B 4¹/₂" and fabric A 2¹/₂" strips as illustrated in Figure 6.

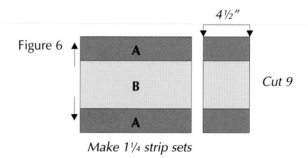

Make 1¹/₄ strip sets

Refer to Figure 7. With right sides together, sew fabrics A and B 2¹/₂" x 8¹/₂" rectangles to these sections *(Figure 5 and 6)* as illustrated. Press seams as arrows indicate.

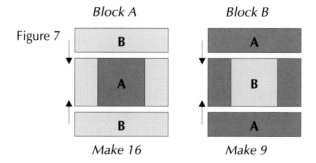

Make 16   Make 9

Setting and Corner Triangles
Refer to Figure 8. With right sides together, sew fabric A 2¹/₂" x 10" rectangle to short side of fabric B setting triangle as illustrated. Gently fingerpress seam as arrow indicates. Sew fabric A 2¹/₂" x 12" rectangle to other short side of setting triangle. Press both seams with an iron as arrows indicate. Using a ruler and rotary cutter, trim off excess fabric so triangle edge is even.

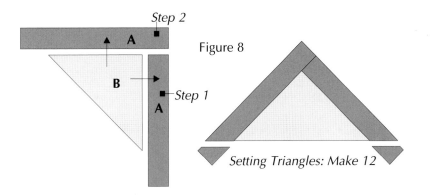

Setting Triangles: Make 12

Sew fabric A 2¹/₂" x 14¹/₂" rectangle to wide side of corner triangle as illustrated in Figure 9. Using ruler and rotary cutter trim strip edges so they are even with triangle.

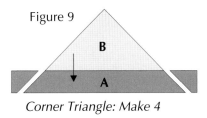

Corner Triangle: Make 4

___

HINT: *To avoid stretching the bias edge in Figure 8 and 9 be sure to sew while keeping the bias edges towards to the feed dogs.*

___

Sew Unit 1 to sides of block A as illustrated in Figure 10. Press seams as arrows indicate.

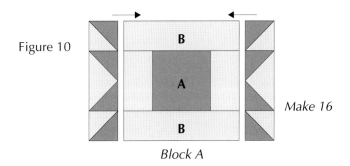

Block A

Sew Units 1 and 2 in alternating order as illustrated in Figure 11 to form rows. Notice that fabric A triangles in Units 1 are pointing up and in Units 2 are pointing down. Sew Blocks A and B together to form rows. Press seams as arrows indicate.

Figure 11

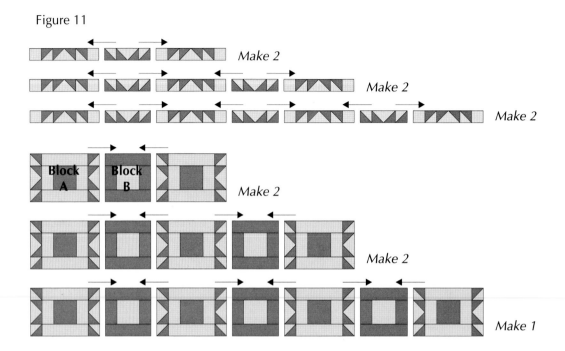

To complete rows, sew units together as illustrated in Figure 12. Press seams as arrows indicate. Sew setting triangles to each end of rows and press.

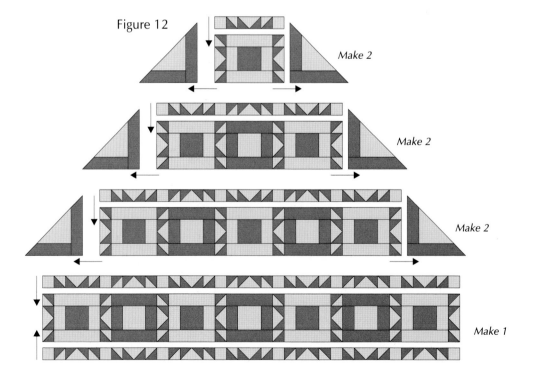

Refer to Figure 13. Sew rows together as illustrated. Press seams as arrows indicate. Sew corner triangles to quilt and press.

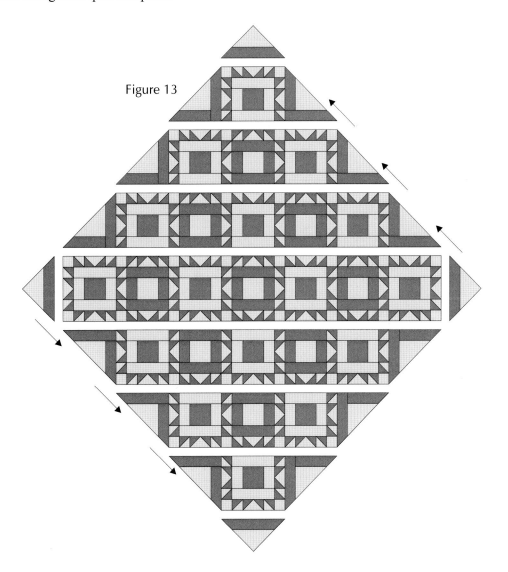

Figure 13

Border
Measure the length of the quilt *(through the center of your quilt)* and piece 2 fabric A border strips (5^1/$_2$") to that measurement. Sew to each side of the quilt and press towards outer edge. Apply border to top and bottom of the quilt using the same technique.

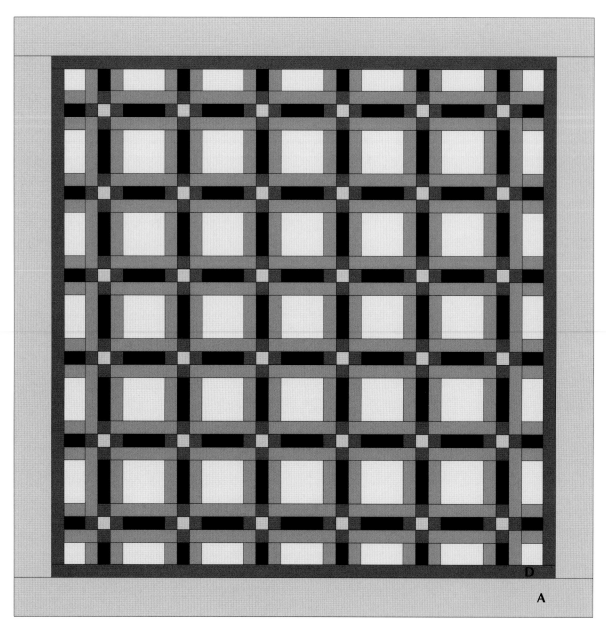

My Secret Garden *approximate size 71" x 71"* • **Wild Thing** *approximate size 63" x 63"*

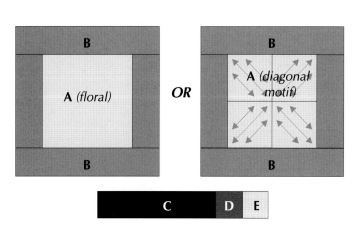

Fabric Requirements: *color photos are on pages 17, 20, 54 and 60*

	My Secret Garden	**Wild Thing**
Fabric A	2 $7/8$* yards	1 $1/4$ yards**
Fabric B	1 $3/4$	2
Fabric C	$7/8$	1 $3/4$
Fabric D	1 $1/8$	$2/3$
Fabric E	$1/4$	$3/4$*

*Includes binding
**Diagonally printed fabric

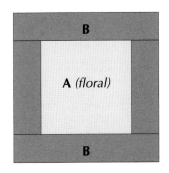

NOTE: *These cutting instructions are based on having 40" of usable fabric width. If your fabric is even slightly wider, you may have strips left over.*

Cutting Instructions for My Secret Garden

Fabric A
5 strips	$5^1/2$" wide	
scraps		Cut into (4) 3" squares

Outer Border
7 strips	6" wide	

Binding
7 strips	$2^1/2$" wide	

Fabric B
10 strips	2" wide	
4 strips	$8^1/2$" wide	Cut into (70) $8^1/2$" x 2" rectangles
scraps		Cut into (4) 2" x $4^1/2$" rectangles
		and (4) 2" x 3" rectangles

Fabric C
3 strips	$5^1/2$" wide	
2 strips	3" wide	

Fabric D
8 strips	2" wide	

Inner Border
6 strips	2" wide	

Fabric E
2 strips	2" wide	Cut into (36) 2" squares

NOTE: *These cutting instructions are based on having 40" of usable fabric width. If your fabric is even slightly wider, you may have strips left over.*

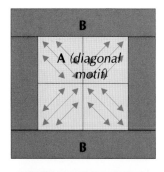

Cutting Instructions for Wild Thing

Fabric A
For best results use a diagonally printed fabric

11 strips	3" wide	Cut into (144) 3" squares

Fabric B

4 strips	8¹/₂" wide	Cut into (70) 8¹/₂" x 2" rectangles
3 strips	5¹/₂" wide	Cut into (50) 5¹/₂" x 2" rectangles
3 strips	3" wide	Cut into (44) 3" x 2" rectangles
scraps		Cut into (4) 4¹/₂" x 2" rectangles

Fabric C

3 strips	5¹/₂" wide
2 strips	3" wide

Outer Border

7 strips	2" wide

Binding

7 strips	2¹/₂" wide

Fabric D

8 strips	2" wide

Fabric E

2 strips	2" wide	Cut into (36) 2" squares

Inner border

7 strips	2" wide

Sewing Instructions for My Secret Garden

With right sides together, sew fabric B 2" and fabric A 5½" strips together lengthwise as illustrated in Figure 1A. Press seams as arrows indicate. Cut pieced A/B strip sets into 5½" and 3" sections.

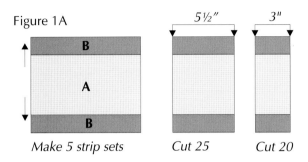

Figure 1A

5½"   3"

B
A
B

Make 5 strip sets   *Cut 25*   *Cut 20*

Sew fabric B 2" x 3" rectangle to one side of four fabric A 3" squares and press seam as arrow indicates in Figure 2A.

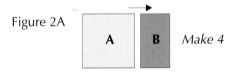

Figure 2A

A   B   *Make 4*

Continue these instructions in paragraph after Figure 3 ☞

Sewing Instructions for Wild Thing

With right sides together, sew fabric A 3" squares together. Position squares so that the diagonally printed motif of the fabric forms a chevron pattern as illustrated in Figure 1. Press seam as pressing arrow indicates.

NOTE: *Leave 4 fabric A 3" squares un-sewn for corner units.*

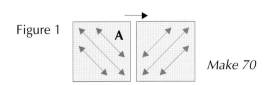

Figure 1

A

Make 70

Sew these units together to make 25 4-patch units joining the chevron patterns as shown in Figure 2. Press seam as arrow indicates.

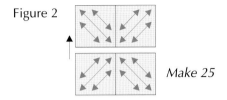

Figure 2

Make 25

Sew fabric B 5½" x 2" and 3" x 2" rectangles to sides of fabric A units as illustrated in Figure 3. Press as arrows indicate.

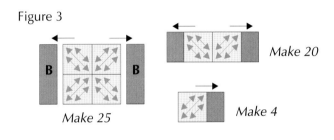

Figure 3

B   B

Make 20

Make 25   *Make 4*

Sew fabric B 8½" x 2" and 4½" x 2" rectangles to fabric A/B units of Figure 1 or 3 as illustrated in Figure 4. Press seams as pressing arrows indicate.

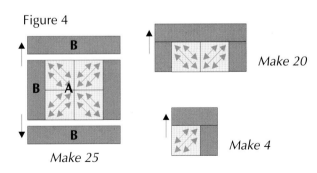

Figure 4

B

B   A

Make 20

B

Make 4

Make 25

With right sides together, sew fabric C 5½" and fabric D 2" strips together lengthwise as illustrated in Figure 5. Repeat, using fabric C 3" strip and fabric D 2" strip. Press seams as arrows indicate. Cut pieced strip sets into 2" sections.

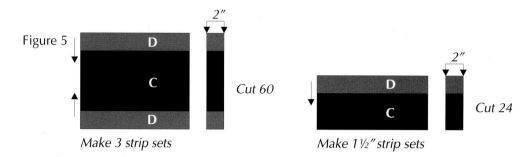

Figure 5

Make 3 strip sets   Cut 60   *Make 1½" strip sets*   Cut 24

Refer to Figure 6. Arrange A/B units in Figure 4, fabric C/D sashing units in Figure 5 and fabric E 2" squares as illustrated. Sew together to form horizontal rows. Press seams as arrows indicate.

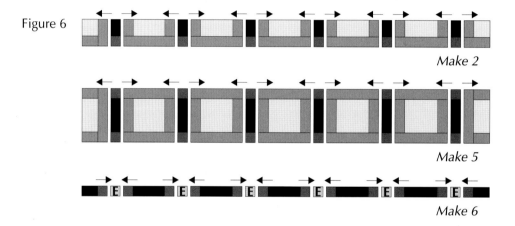

Figure 6

Make 2

Make 5

Make 6

Refer to Figure 7 and sew rows together as illustrated. Press as arrows indicate.

Figure 7

Border

My Secret Garden

Measure the length of your quilt *(through the center of your quilt)* and piece 2 fabric D (2") inner border strips to that measurement. Sew to each side of the quilt and press seams towards outer edge. Apply inner border to top and bottom of the quilt using the same technique. Repeat these steps using fabric A (6") outer border.

Wild Thing

Measure the length of your quilt *(through the center of your quilt)* and piece 2 fabric E (2") inner border strips to that measurement. Sew to each side of the quilt and press seams towards outer edge. Apply inner border to top and bottom of the quilt using the same technique. Repeat these steps using fabric C (2") outer border.

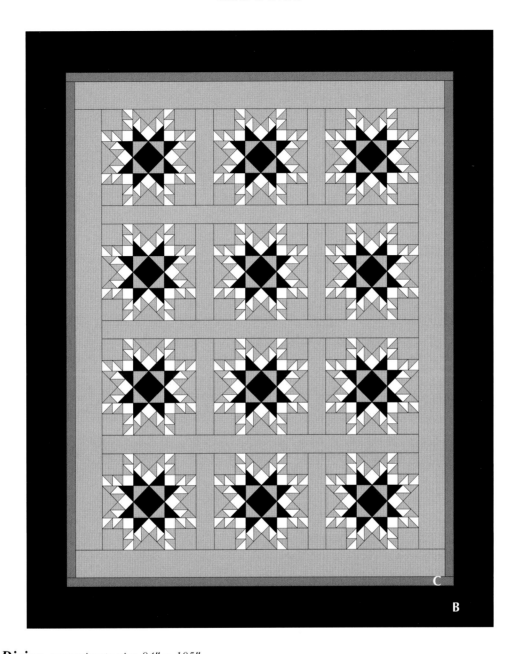

Simple & Divine *approximate size 84" x 105"*

This feathered star design does not use set-in seams!

Fabric Requirements: *color photos are on pages 40 and 47*

Fabric A	5 yards
Fabric B	$2^7/8$*
Fabric C	$1^3/8$
Fabric D	$^3/4$
Fabric E	$1^3/4$

*Includes binding

NOTE: *These cutting instructions are based on having 40" of usable fabric width. If your fabric is even slightly wider, you may have strips left over.*

IMPORTANT: *Label your pieces as you cut them. Some of the sizes are very similar and it's easy to mix them up.*

Cutting Instructions for Simple & Divine

Fabric A

◣ 8 strips $2^7/8$" wide   Cut into (96) $2^7/8$" squares
◣ 8 strips   3" wide   Cut into (96) 3" squares
   6 strips $4^1/2$" wide   Cut into (48) $4^1/2$" squares
   3 strips $7^1/4$" wide   Cut into (12) $7^1/4$" squares

Sashing
9 strips $3^1/2$" wide   Leave 5 strips whole
     Cut into (8) $3^1/2$" x $18^1/2$" rectangles

Inner border
8 strips $4^1/2$" wide

Fabric B
2 strips $6^1/2$" wide   Cut into (12) $6^1/2$" squares

Outer border
9 strips $6^1/2$" wide
Binding
9 strips $2^1/2$" wide

Fabric C
5 strips $3^1/2$" wide   Cut into (48) $3^1/2$" squares

Inner Border
9 strips $2^1/2$" wide

Fabric D
5 strips $3^7/8$" wide   Cut into (48) $3^7/8$" squares

Fabric E
   3 strips $2^1/2$" wide   Cut into (48) $2^1/2$" squares
   4 strips $2^5/8$" wide   Cut into (48) $2^5/8$" squares
◣ 8 strips $2^7/8$" wide   Cut into (96) $2^7/8$" squares
◣ 4 strips   3" wide   Cut into (48) 3 " squares

◣ *Do NOT cut these strips if you plan on making half square triangles by drawing a grid or using products such as Triangle Paper™ or Triangles on a Roll™*

Sewing Instructions

Draw a diagonal line on the wrong side of fabric C
3¹/₂" squares *(Using the Angler 2 or drawing a sewing
guide onto your machine will eliminate this step.)*

Figure 1

*48 fabric C
3½" squares*

Starting at one corner, with right sides together, place
fabric C 3¹/₂" square on top of a fabric B 6¹/₂" square.
Stitch on the pencil line. Press seam towards outer
edge and then trim to measure ¹/₄" as illustrated in
Figure 2. Complete each corner before going on to
the next.

Figure 2

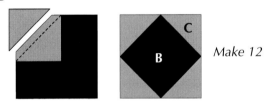

Make 12

Use your favorite technique to make half square
triangles or use the following method.

Place fabric A and E 2⁷/₈" squares right sides together.
Cut them in half diagonally. Sew pairs of A and E
triangles together on the wide edge. Press seam
towards darker fabric and trim off dog ears.

Figure 3

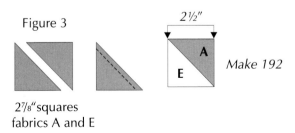

2½"

Make 192

2⁷/₈" squares
fabrics A and E

Sew half square triangles together as illustrated in
Figure 4. Notice that in Unit 1 the diagonal seams
between A and E rise to the right and in Unit 2 they rise
to the left. Press seams as arrows indicate.

Figure 4

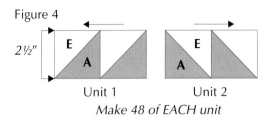

2½"

Unit 1   Unit 2

Make 48 of EACH unit

Sew fabric E 2¹/₂" square to Unit 1 as illustrated in
Figure 5. Press seam as arrow indicates.

Figure 5

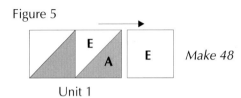

Make 48

Unit 1

Sew Units 1 and 2 to fabric A 4¹/₂" square as illustrated
in Figure 6. Press seams as arrows indicate.

Figure 6

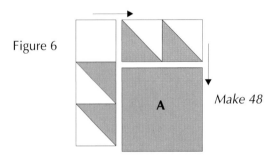

Make 48

Refer to Figure 7. Place fabric A and E 3" squares right
sides together. Cut them in half diagonally. Sew pairs of
A and E triangles together on the wide edge. Refer to
Figure 7. Press seam towards darker fabric and trim
off dog ears.

Figure 7

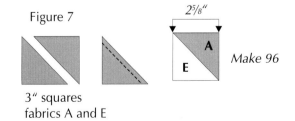

2⁵/₈"

Make 96

3" squares
fabrics A and E

Cut fabric A 3" squares in half diagonally into triangles. Sew triangles onto the $2^5/8$" half square triangles as illustrated in Figure 8.

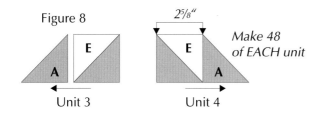

Figure 8

$2^5/8$"

Make 48 of EACH unit

Unit 3

Unit 4

IMPORTANT: *Handle Units 3 and 4 gently, especially when pressing. Do not stretch the bias edge of the triangle.*

Sew a fabric E $2^5/8$" square onto Unit 4 as illustrated in Figure 9. Press seam as arrow indicates.

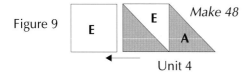

Figure 9

Make 48

Unit 4

 Cut fabric A $7^1/4$" squares in half diagonally twice into quarter triangles.

Sew Units 3 and 4 to fabric A quarter triangle as illustrated in Figure 10. Press seams as arrows indicate.

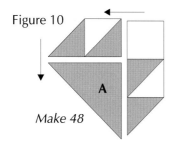

Figure 10

Make 48

 Cut fabric D $3^7/8$" squares in half diagonally.

Refer to Figure 11. Sew the wide edge of fabric D triangle as illustrated. Press seam toward fabric D as arrow indicates. Apply another triangle to the other side.

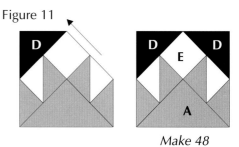

Figure 11

Make 48

Sew units into 3 horizontal rows as illustrated in Figure 12. Press seams as arrows indicate. Complete the block by sewing the rows together. Press seams as arrows indicate.

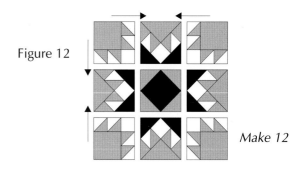

Figure 12

Make 12

Refer to Figure 13. Sew fabric A $3^1/2$" x $18^1/2$" sashing rectangles onto left and right sides of 4 blocks. Press seams towards sashing. Make rows by sewing a block onto each side of these units.

Measure the length of these rows and piece 3 sashing strips ($3^1/2$") to that length. Sew sashing strips between 4 rows. Press seams towards sashing.

IMPORTANT NOTE: *If the length of the rows are slightly different, compute their average length and piece all fabric A strips to that value.*

Figure 13

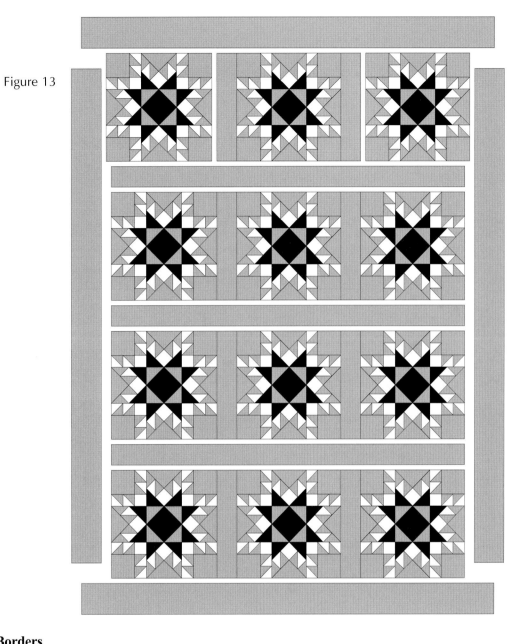

Borders

Measure length of quilt *(through the center of your quilt)* and piece 2 fabric A ($4^{1}/_{2}$")
inner border strips to that measurement. Apply to each side of quilt and press seams
towards outer edge. Apply inner border to top and bottom of the quilt using the same
technique.

Repeat these steps and apply fabric C ($2^{1}/_{2}$") accent border followed by fabric B ($6^{1}/_{2}$")
outer border.

Hog Heaven • Fitzwilliam & Ross approximate size 75" x 88"

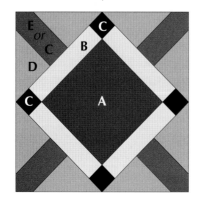

Fabric Requirements: *color photos are on pages 36, 39, 53 and 62*

	Hog Heaven	Fitzwilliam & Ross
Fabric A	3¹/₃* yards	2 ¹/₄ yards
Fabric B	1¹/₄	1¹/₄
Fabric C	1³/₄	1⁷/₈
Fabric D	2³/₄	2³/₄
Fabric E	—	1¹/₂

Includes binding

NOTE: *These cutting instructions*
are based on having 40" of usable
fabric width. If your fabric is even
slightly wider, you may have strips
left over.

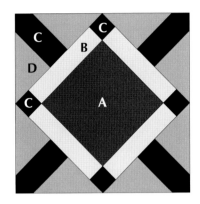

Cutting Instructions for Hog Heaven

Fabric A

5 strips	6" wide	Cut into (30) 6" squares

Border

8 strips	6" wide

Binding

10 strips	2$\frac{1}{2}$" wide

Fabric B *Use these cutting instructions if your fabric is NOT directional or angularly printed such as a plaid or check. If you are using checks or plaids, refer to the special cutting instructions below.*

20 strips	1$\frac{3}{4}$" wide	Cut into (120) 1$\frac{3}{4}$" x 6" rectangles

Cutting instructions for checked or plaid fabric:

Cut 2 sections 21" long from your yardage. Open fabric so you are working with a single layer. Trim off selvage by lining up your ruler evenly against a row of checks. Cut the indicated strips from this edge, squaring up your fabric often. *(These are referred to as short strips because they are equal to one half of a normal strip).*

40 short strips	1$\frac{3}{4}$" wide	Cut into (120) 1$\frac{3}{4}$" x 6" rectangles

Fabric C

6 strip	1$\frac{3}{4}$" wide	Cut into (120) 1$\frac{3}{4}$" squares
4 strips	10" wide	Cut into (60) 10" x 2$\frac{1}{2}$" rectangles
2 strips	1$\frac{1}{2}$" wide	Cut into (42) 1$\frac{1}{2}$" squares

Fabric D

9 strips	5$\frac{5}{8}$" wide	Cut into (60) 5$\frac{5}{8}$" squares

Sashing

24 strips	1$\frac{1}{2}$" wide	Cut into (71) rectangles 1$\frac{1}{2}$" by the average measurement of your blocks

Freezer paper   (60) 3" squares and *cut in half diagonally once*

NOTE: *These cutting instructions are based on having 40" of usable fabric width. If your fabric is even slightly wider, you may have strips left over.*

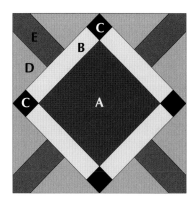

Cutting Instructions for Fitzwilliam & Ross

Fabric A

5 strips	6" wide	Cut into (30) 6" squares

Inner border

8 strips	4$\frac{1}{2}$" wide

Fabric B

20 strips	1$\frac{3}{4}$" wide	Cut into (120) 1$\frac{3}{4}$" x 6" rectangles

---

Fabric C

6 strips	1$\frac{3}{4}$" wide	Cut into (120) 1$\frac{3}{4}$" squares

Outer border

9 strips	2$\frac{1}{2}$" wide

Binding

10 strips	2$\frac{1}{2}$" wide

Fabric D

9 strips	5$\frac{5}{8}$" wide	Cut into (60) 5$\frac{5}{8}$" squares

Sashing

24 strips	1$\frac{1}{2}$" wide	Cut into (71) rectangles 1$\frac{1}{2}$" by the average measurement of your blocks

---

Fabric E

4 strips	10" wide	Cut into (60) 10" x 2$\frac{1}{2}$" rectangles
2 strips	1$\frac{1}{2}$" wide	Cut into (42) 1$\frac{1}{2}$" squares

---

Freezer paper   (60) 3" squares *cut in half diagonally once*

Sewing Instructions

Refer to Figure 1. Sew fabric B $1^3/4$" x 6" strips to sides of fabric A 6" square as illustrated. Press seams as arrows indicate.

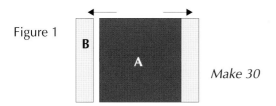

Figure 1   B   A   *Make 30*

Refer to Figure 2. Sew fabric C $1^3/4$" square onto each end of the remaining fabric B $1^3/4$" x 6" rectangles. Press seams as arrows indicate.

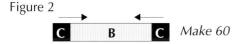

Figure 2   C   B   C   *Make 60*

Sew units together to form block as illustrated in Figure 3. Press seams as arrows indicate.

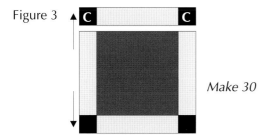

Figure 3   C   C   *Make 30*

Refer to Figure 4. With **RIGHT** sides together, lightly press fabric D $5^5/8$" squares in half along the diagonal.

With **WRONG** sides together lightly press fabric C *(for Hog Heaven)* or E *(for Fitzwilliam & Ross)* 10" x $2^1/2$" rectangles in half.

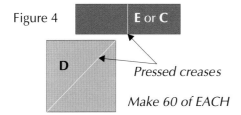

Figure 4   E or C   D   *Pressed creases*

Make 60 of EACH

Refer to Figure 5. Cut fabric D $5^5/8$" squares in half along the diagonal. Notice that your cut is going across the pressed crease.

Figure 5

With right sides together, align crease lines of fabric E or C 10" x $2^1/2$" rectangles and fabric D triangles. Secure alignment with pins. Sew together as illustrated in Figure 6. Press seams as arrows indicate.

Designer Tip: *If you pressed as instructed, fabric D triangle and fabric E or C rectangle should nestle easily into each other.*

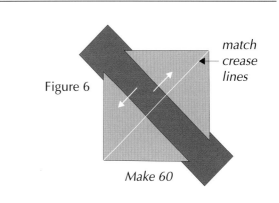

match crease lines

Figure 6   *Make 60*

Designer Tip: *Place fabric pieces with bias edge next to the feed dogs when sewing.*

Fold pieced unit in Figure 6 in half along the diagonal. Fingerpress it in place. Accuracy is very important in this step. Using a ruler and rotary cutter, trim off excess fabric as Figure 7 illustrates.

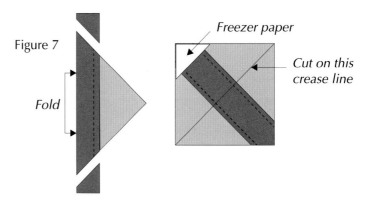

Turn unit so wrong side is facing you. Press freezer paper triangles onto corners, shiny side down, as illustrated in Figure 7. This will stabilize the bias edges while you are working. Do NOT skip this step.

Cut these pieced squares in half along the diagonal crease line to form triangles.

Refer to Figure 8. With wrong sides together, very lightly press block in half in both directions. Use these crease lines to align each side of the block to the center of a pieced triangle. Sew side of block and triangle together. Press seam towards outer edge as you work. Complete each side before going on to the next.

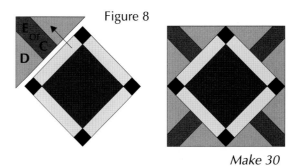

Make 30

Trim dog ears from finished block. If necessary, trim edges to even up the block but be sure not to cut anything off the corners and only the slightest slivers off the block itself.

Measure blocks and cut (71) fabric D $1^1/2$" sashing strips to the average of those measurements. Sew sashing strips between blocks as well as on each end of row as illustrated in Figure 9. Press seams towards sashing as arrows indicate.

Designer Tip: *Lightly press sashing strips in half. Align center of the block to this crease. This is an easy way to line up your blocks.*

Figure 9

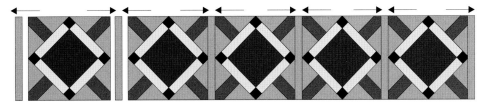

Make 6

Sew fabric E or C 1¹/₂" squares and remaining fabric D sashing strips together as illustrated in Figure 10. Press seams as arrows indicate.

Figure 10

Make 7

To assemble the quilt, sew pieced sashing to the top, bottom and in-between rows and press. Carefully remove freezer paper from corners.

Borders
Hog Heaven
Measure the length of your quilt *(through the center of the quilt)* and piece 2 fabric A (6") inner border strips to that measurement. Sew to each side of the quilt and press seam towards outer edge. Apply inner border strips to top and bottom using the same technique.

Fitzwilliam & Ross
Measure the length of your quilt *(through the center of the quilt)* and piece 2 fabric A (4¹/₂") inner border strips to that measurement. Sew to each side of the quilt and press seam towards outer edge. Apply inner border strips to top and bottom using the same technique.

Repeat these steps for fabric C (2¹/₂") outer border.

Argyle approximate size 64" x 64"

Fabric Requirements: *color photos are on pages 28 and 46*

Fabric A	1¼ yards
Fabric B	2¼*
Fabric C	1¼
Fabric D	1¾
Fabric E	⅓

Includes binding

NOTE: These cutting instructions are based on having 40" of usable fabric width. If your fabric is even slightly wider, you may have strips left over.

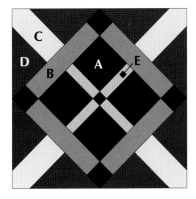

Cutting Instructions for Argyle

Fabric A
6 strips	$2^7/8$" wide	
3 strips	$1^3/4$" wide	
1 strip	$1^1/4$" wide	

Inner border 2
6 strips	2" wide

Fabric B
4 strips	6" wide	Leave 2 strips whole
		Cut into (32) 6" x $1^3/4$" rectangles

Outer border
7 strips	4" wide

Binding
7 strips	$2^1/2$" wide

Fabric C
2 strips	10" wide	Cut into (32) 10" x $2^1/2$" rectangles
1 strip	$1^1/2$" wide	Cut into (25) $1^1/2$" squares

Inner border 1
6 strips	2" wide

Fabric D
6 strips	$5^5/8$" wide	Cut into (32) $5^5/8$" squares

Sashing
14 strips	$1^1/2$" wide	Cut into (40) rectangles $1^1/2$" by the average measurement of your blocks

Fabric E
3 strips	$1^1/4$" wide	
1 strip	$2^7/8$" wide	

Freezer paper   (32) 3" squares and *cut in half diagonally once*

Sewing Instructions

Sew fabric A 2⅞" strips and fabric E 1¼" strip together lengthwise as illustrated in Figure 1. Press seams as arrows indicate. Cut into 2⅞" sections.

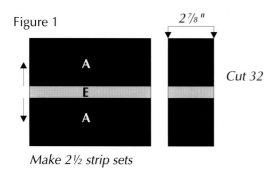

Figure 1

2⅞"

Cut 32

Make 2½ strip sets

Sew fabric E 2⅞" strips and fabric A 1¼" strip together lengthwise as illustrated in Figure 2. Press seams as arrows indicate. Cut into 1¼" sections.

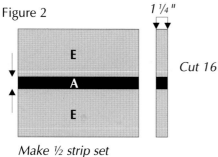

Figure 2

1¼"

Cut 16

Make ½ strip set

Sew sections together to form block as illustrated in Figure 3. Press seams as arrows indicate.

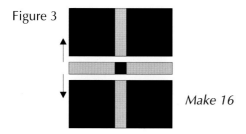

Figure 3

Make 16

Sew fabric B 6" x 1¾" rectangles onto sides of block as illustrated in Figure 4. Press seams as arrows indicate.

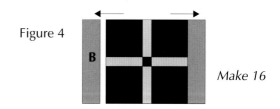

Figure 4

B

Make 16

Sew fabric B 6" strip and fabric A 1¾" strips together lengthwise as illustrated in Figure 5. Press seams as arrows indicate. Cut into 1¾" sections.

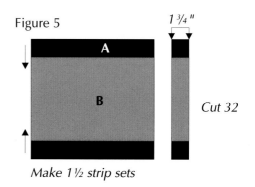

Figure 5

1¾"

A

B

Cut 32

Make 1½ strip sets

Sew these A/B units to top and bottom of block as Figure 6 illustrates. Press as arrows indicate.

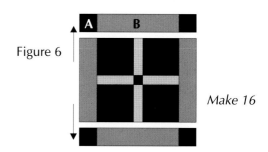

Figure 6

A   B

Make 16

Refer to Figure 7. With **RIGHT** sides together, press fabric D 5⅝" squares in half along the diagonal.

With **WRONG** sides together press fabric C 10" x 2½" rectangles in half.

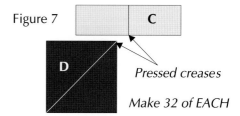

Figure 7

C

D

Pressed creases

Make 32 of EACH

Refer to Figure 8. Cut fabric D 5⅝" squares in half along the diagonal. Notice that your cut is going across the pressed crease.

Figure 8

With right sides together, align crease lines of fabric C rectangle and fabric D triangles. Secure alignment with pins. Sew together as illustrated in Figure 9. Press seams as arrows indicate.

Designer Tip: *If you pressed as instructed, fabric D square and fabric C rectangle should nestle easily into each other.*

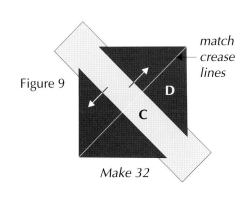

Figure 9

match
crease
lines

D

C

Make 32

Designer Tip: *Place fabric pieces with bias edge next to the feed dogs when sewing.*

Fold pieced unit in half along the diagonal. Fingerpress it in place. Accuracy is very important in this step. Using a ruler and rotary cutter, trim off excess fabric as Figure 10 illustrates.

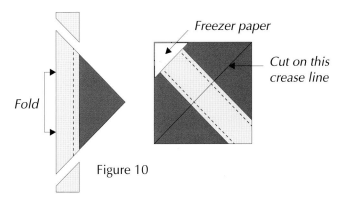

Freezer paper

Cut on this crease line

Fold

Figure 10

Turn unit so that wrong side is facing you. Press freezer paper triangles onto corners, shiny side down, as illustrated in Figure 10. This will stabilize the bias edges while you are working. Do NOT skip this step.

Cut these C/D units in half along the diagonal crease line to form triangles.

Refer to Figure 11. With wrong sides together, very lightly press block in half in both directions. Use these crease lines to align each side of the block to the center of a pieced triangle. Sew side of block and triangle together. Press seam towards outer edge as you work. Complete each side before going on to the next.

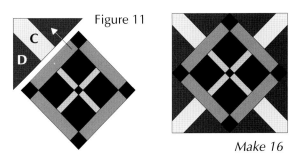

Figure 11

C

D

Make 16

Trim dog ears from finished block. If necessary, trim edges to even up the block but be sure not to cut anything off the corners and only the slightest slivers off the block itself.

Measure blocks and cut 40 fabric D 1½" sashing strips to the average length of those measurements. Sew sashing strips between blocks as well as on each end of row as illustrated in Figure 12. Press seams towards sashing as arrows indicate.

Designer Tip: *Lightly press sashing strips in half. Align center of the block to this crease. This is an easy way to line up your blocks.*

Figure 12

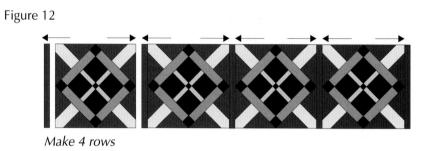

Make 4 rows

Sew fabric C 1¹/₂" squares and remaining fabric D sashing strips together as illustrated in Figure 13. Press seams as arrows indicate.

Figure 13

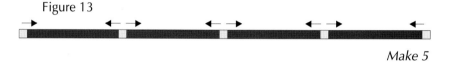

Make 5

To assemble the quilt, sew pieced sashing to the top, bottom and between rows and press. Carefully remove freezer paper from corners of the blocks.

Border

Measure the length of your quilt *(through the center of the quilt)* and piece 2 fabric C (2") inner border 1 strips to that measurement. Sew to each side of the quilt and press seam towards outer edge. Apply inner border 1 strips to top and bottom using the same technique.

Repeat these steps using fabric A (2") strips for inner border 2.

Repeat, this time using fabric B (4") strips for the outer border.

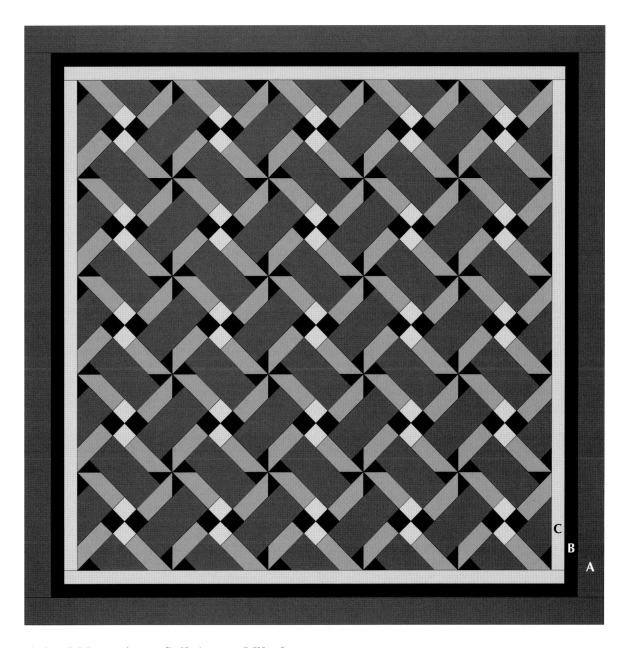

Animal Magnetism • Sail Away • Mikado *approximate size 71" x 71"*

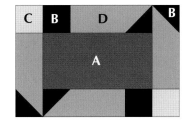

Fabric Requirements: *color photos are on pages 11, 12, 23, 43, 44 and 50*

Fabric A	$3^3/4$* yards
Fabric B	$1^1/2$
Fabric C	1
Fabric D	$1^1/2$

Includes binding

NOTE: *These cutting instructions are based on having 40" of usable fabric width. If your fabric is even slightly wider, you may have strips left over.*

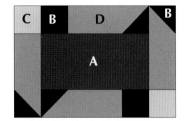

Cutting Instructions for Animal Magnetism • Sail Away • Mikado

Fabric A

5 strips	8½" wide	Cut into (40) 8½" x 4½" rectangles

Setting triangles

2 strips	9¾" wide	Cut into (5) 9¾" squares and *cut in half diagonally twice*

Outer border

8 strips	4½" wide

Binding

8 strips	2½" wide

Fabric B

9 strips	2½" wide	Leave 3 strips whole
		Cut into (90) 2½" squares
1 strip	3⅝" wide	Cut into (10) 3⅝" squares

Inner border 2

7 strips	2½" wide

Fabric C

4 strips	2½" wide	Leave 3 strips whole
		Cut into (10) 2½" squares

Inner border 1

7 strips	2½" wide

Fabric D

5 strips	6½" wide	
4 strips	2½" wide	Cut into (20) 2½" x 7½" rectangles

Sewing Instructions

Sew fabric C 2¹/₂" and fabric D 6¹/₂" strips together lengthwise as illustrated in Figure 1. Press seams as arrows indicate. Cut pieced strip sets into 2¹/₂" sections. Repeat, using fabric B 2¹/₂" and fabric D 6¹/₂" strips.

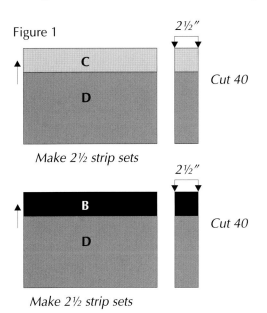

Figure 1

2¹/₂"

C

D

Cut 40

Make 2½ strip sets

2¹/₂"

B

D

Cut 40

Make 2½ strip sets

Using a sharp pencil, draw a diagonal line on the wrong side of 80 fabric B 2¹/₂" squares. *(Using the Angler 2 or drawing a sewing guide onto your machine will eliminate this step.)*

Figure 2

80 fabric B 2½" squares

With right sides together, position a fabric B 2¹/₂" square on the end of fabric C/D and B/D units as illustrated in Figure 3. Stitch on the pencil line. Press seam towards outer edge and trim seam allowance to measure ¹/₄".

Figure 3

C   D   B   *Make 40*

B   D   *Make 40*

Sew fabric B/D units to fabric A 8¹/₂" x 4¹/₂" rectangle as illustrated in Figure 4. Press seams as arrows indicate.

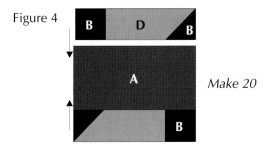

Figure 4

B   D   B

A

Make 20

B

Sew fabric C/D/B units to pieced blocks and also to fabric A 8¹/₂" x 4¹/₂" rectangles as illustrated in Figure 5. Press seams as arrows indicate.

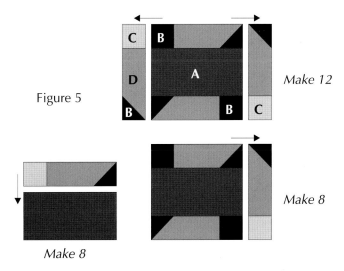

Figure 5

C   B

D   A

B   B   C

Make 12

Make 8

Make 8

Using a sharp pencil, draw a diagonal line on the wrong side of 10 fabric B 3⁵/₈" squares. *(Do this even if you usually don't draw pencil sewing lines.)*

Figure 6

10 fabric B 3⁵/₈" squares

Cut these squares in half diagonally as illustrated in Figure 7. Notice that the cut is going across the pencil line.

Figure 7

Pencil line

Setting triangles
With right sides together, place this fabric B triangle onto the LEFT corner of a fabric A setting triangle as illustrated in Figure 8. Stitch on the pencil line. Very carefully, fingerpress seam allowance towards outer edge and then trim to measure $1/4$".

Figure 8

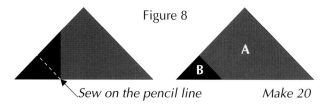

Sew on the pencil line   *Make 20*

Designer Tip: *Make sure that the angles of fabric B triangle are oriented exactly as illustrated in Figure 8. Exercise care when handling and pressing these setting triangles so they do not get stretched out of shape.*

Refer to Figure 9. Sew fabric C and B $2^{1}/2$" squares onto end of fabric D $2^{1}/2$" x $7^{1}/2$" rectangles. Press seams as arrows indicate.

Figure 9

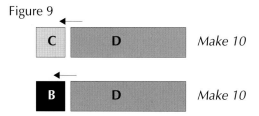

Make 10

Make 10

Sew these units to short side of setting triangles as illustrated in Figure 10. Press seams as arrows indicate. Using a ruler and rotary cutter, trim off excess fabric so triangle edge is even.

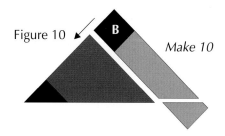

Figure 10   *Make 10*

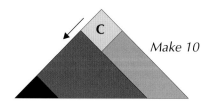

Make 10

Corner triangles
To make corner triangle, sew 2 setting triangles together as illustrated in Figure 11. Press seams as arrows indicate. Be sure to handle bias edges with care.

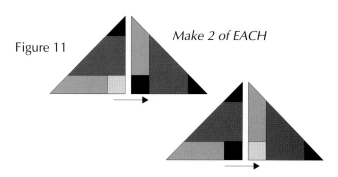

Figure 11   *Make 2 of EACH*

To assemble the quilt, arrange blocks, setting triangles, corner triangles and fabric A $8^{1}/2$" x $4^{1}/2$" rectangles as illustrated in Figure 12. Sew pieces into rows. Press seams as arrows indicate. Sew rows together and press.

Borders
Measure the length of your quilt *(through the center of your quilt)* and piece 2 fabric C inner border 1 strips ($2^{1}/2$") to that measurement. Sew to each side of the quilt and press towards outer edge. Apply inner border 1 to top and bottom of the quilt using the same technique.

Repeat these steps for inner border 2, this time using fabric B ($2^{1}/2$") strips.

Repeat these steps, this time using fabric A ($4^{1}/2$") strips for the outer border.

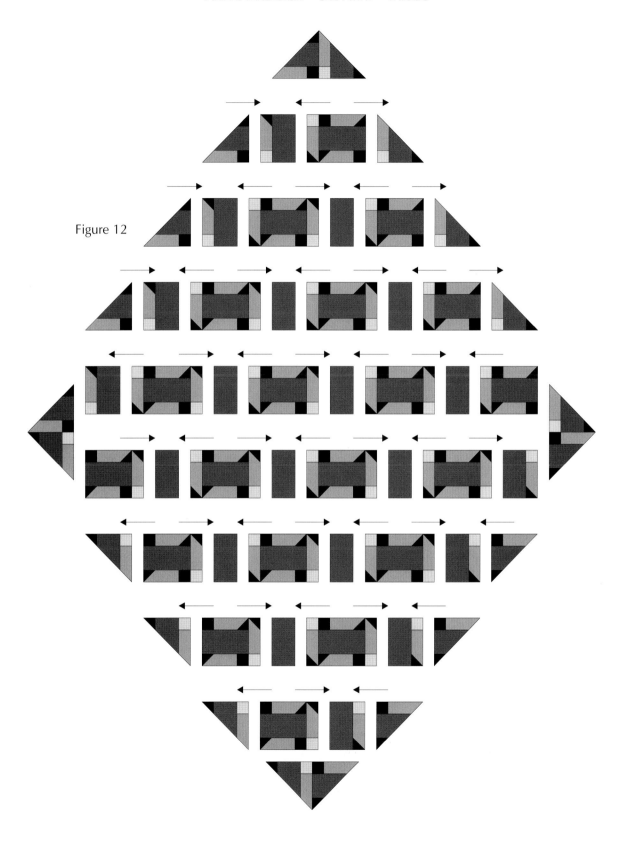

Figure 12

Italian Tile • Fruit Salad *approximate size 52" x 64"*

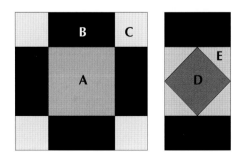

Fabric Requirements: *color photos are on pages 9, 18, 49 and 61*

Fabric A	³/₄ yards
Fabric B	1¹/₂ *(add ¹/₄ yard for stripes)*
Fabric C	¹/₂
Fabric D	³/₄**
Fabric E	³/₄ OR 3 pieces ³/₈ yard each
Fabric F	1¹/₂*

*Includes binding

**This yardage does not allow for fussy cutting. You will need enough yardage to cut 32 (4¹/₂") motifs.

NOTE: These cutting instructions are based on having 40" of usable fabric width. If your fabric is even slightly wider, you may have strips left over.

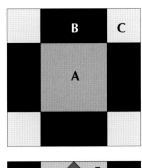

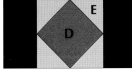

Cutting Instructions for Italian Tile • Fruit Salad

Fabric A

4 strips	4¹/2" wide	Leave 2 strips whole
		Cut into (16) 4¹/2" squares

Fabric B *Use these cutting instructions if your fabric is **NOT** directional. If you are using striped fabric, refer to the special cutting instructions below.*

4 strips	2¹/2" wide	
7 strips	4¹/2" wide	Leave 2¹/2 strips whole
		Cut into (72) 4¹/2" x 2¹/2" rectangles

Cutting Instructions for striped fabric:

Cut 2 sections 21" long from your yardage. Open fabric so you are working with a single layer. Trim off selvage by lining up your ruler evenly against one of the stripes. Cut the indicated short strips from this edge, squaring up your fabric often. *(These are referred to as short strips because they are equal to one half of a normal strip.)*

14 short strips	4¹/2" wide *(21" long)*	Leave 5 short strips whole
		Cut into (72) 4¹/2" x 2¹/2" rectangles

from yardage cut:

4 strips	2¹/2" wide

Fabric C

5 strips	2¹/2" wide

Fabric D

*4 strips	4¹/2" wide	Cut into (32) 4¹/2" squares **OR**
		Fussy cut (32) 4¹/2" squares

**Do NOT cut these strips if you are fussy cutting the 4¹/2" squares*

Fabric E

8 strips	2¹/2" wide	Cut into (128) 2¹/2" squares

Fabric F

Border

6 strips	4¹/2" wide

Binding

6 strips	2¹/2" wide

Sewing Instructions

With right sides together, sew fabric B $2^{1}/2$" and fabric A $4^{1}/2$" strips together lengthwise as illustrated in Figure 1. Press seams as arrows indicate. Cut strip sets into $4^{1}/2$" sections.

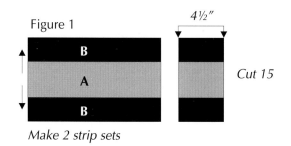

Figure 1

$4^{1}/2$"

B
A
B

Cut 15

Make 2 strip sets

With right sides together, sew fabric C $2^{1}/2$" and fabric B $4^{1}/2$" strips together lengthwise as illustrated in Figure 2. Press seams as arrows indicate. Cut strip sets into $2^{1}/2$" sections.

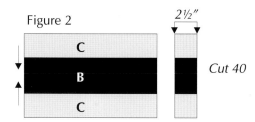

Figure 2

$2^{1}/2$"

C
B
C

Cut 40

Make 2½ strip sets OR 5 short strip sets

Sew these units together as illustrated in Figure 3. Press seams as arrows indicate.

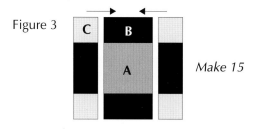

Figure 3

C B

A

Make 15

Draw a diagonal line on the wrong side of 128 fabric E $2^{1}/2$" squares. *(Using the Angler 2 or drawing a sewing guide onto your machine will eliminate this step.)*

Figure 4

*128 fabric E
$2^{1}/2$" squares*

Refer to Figure 5. With right sides together, position a fabric E $2^{1}/2$" square on a corner of a fabric D $4^{1}/2$" square. Stitch on the pencil line. Press seam allowance towards outer edge and then trim to measure $^{1}/4$". Repeat these steps for all corners.

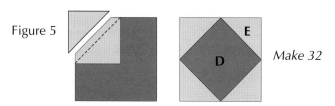

Figure 5

E
D

Make 32

Sew fabric B $4^{1}/2$" x $2^{1}/2$" rectangles onto fabric D/E units and fabric A $4^{1}/2$" square as illustrated in Figure 6. Press seams as arrows indicate.

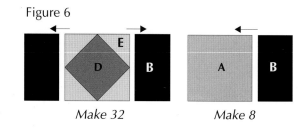

Figure 6

E
D B

A B

Make 32   *Make 8*

Sew fabric B/C unit onto a fabric B/D/E unit as illustrated in Figure 7. Press seam as arrow indicates.

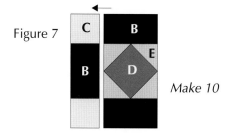

Figure 7

C B

B D E

Make 10

Refer to Figure 8. Sew the units you've made and fabric A $4^{1}/2$" squares into rows as illustrated. Press seams as arrows indicate.

Sew rows together. Press seams as arrows indicate in Figure 8.

Figure 8

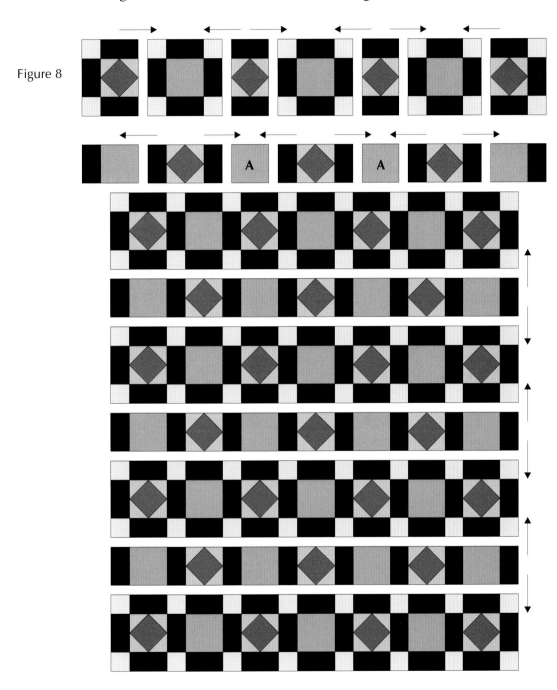

Measure the length of your quilt *(through the center of your quilt)* and piece 2 fabric F border strips (4^1/$_2$") to that measurement. Sew to each side of the quilt and press towards outer edge. Apply border to top and bottom of the quilt using the same technique.

Lilacs & Lace *approximate size 73" x 73"*

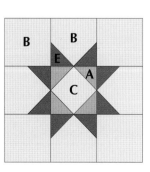

Block B

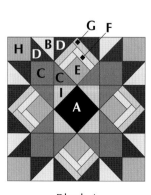

Block A

Fabric Requirements: *color photos are on pages 27 and 59*

Fabric A	$3^1/2$* yards
Fabric B	$1^7/8$
Fabric C	1
Fabric D	$1^1/4$
Fabric E	$^1/2$
Fabric F	$^1/2$
Fabric G	$^5/8$
Fabric H	$^1/3$
Fabric I	$^1/3$
Fabric J	$^1/4$

Cutting Instructions for Lilacs & Lace

NOTE: *These cutting instructions are based on having 40" of usable fabric width. If your fabric is even slightly wider, you may have strips left over.*

Block A

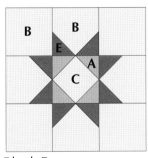

Block B

NOTE: The arrow mark ■

■ *Do NOT cut these strips if you plan on making half square triangles by using products such as Triangle Paper™ or Triangles on a Roll™*

* *These pieces will be used for foundation piecing and do not need to be cut with absolute precision.*

Fabric A
Block A

1 strip	$4^{1}/2$" wide	Cut into (9) $4^{1}/2$" squares

Block B

1 strip	$2^{1}/2$" wide	Cut into (16) $2^{1}/2$" squares

Setting triangles

2 squares	$21^{1}/4$" square	*Cut in half diagonally twice*

Corner triangles

2 squares	$12^{1}/2$" square	*Cut in half diagonally once*

Outer border

8 strips	5" wide

Binding

8 strips	$2^{1}/2$" wide

Fabric B
Block A

■ 3 strips	$2^{7}/8$" wide	Cut into (36) $2^{7}/8$" squares

Block B

4 strips	$4^{1}/2$" wide	Cut into (32) $4^{1}/2$" squares

Sashing

12 strips	$2^{1}/2$" wide	Cut into (36) $2^{1}/2$" x $12^{1}/2$" rectangles

Fabric C
Block A

3 strips	$2^{1}/2$" wide	Cut into (36) $2^{1}/2$" squares
*4 strips	4" wide	Cut into (36) 4" squares and *cut in half diagonally once*

Block B

1 strips	$4^{1}/2$" wide	Cut into (4) $4^{1}/2$" squares

Fabric D
Block A

■ 3 strips	$2^{7}/8$" wide	Cut into (36) $2^{7}/8$" squares
*4 strips	4" wide	Cut into (36) 4" squares and *cut in half diagonally once*

Inner Border

7 strips	$1^{1}/2$" wide

Fabric E
Block A

*3 strips	$2^{1}/2$" wide	Cut into (36) $2^{1}/2$" squares

Block B

2 strips	$2^{1}/2$" wide	Cut into (32) $2^{1}/2$" squares

Fabric F
Block A
| *4 strips | 3¹/4" wide | Cut into (72) 3¹/4" x 1³/4" rectangles |

Fabric G
Block A
| *4 strips | 3³/4" wide | Cut into (72) 3³/4" x 1³/4" rectangles |

Fabric H
| 3 strips | 2¹/2" wide | Cut into (36) 2¹/2" squares |

Fabric I
| 3 strips | 2¹/2" wide | Cut into (36) 2¹/2" squares |

Fabric J
| 2 strip | 2¹/2" wide | Cut into (24) 2¹/2" squares |

Sewing Instructions
Block A

Draw a diagonal line on the wrong side of fabric I 2¹/2" squares. *(Using the Angler 2 or drawing a sewing guide onto your machine will eliminate this step.)*

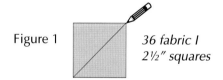

Figure 1   *36 fabric I*
2½" squares

Refer to Figure 2. With right sides together, place a fabric I 2¹/2" square on a corner of fabric A 4¹/2" square. Stitch on the pencil line. Press seam towards outer edge and then trim seam allowance to measure ¹/4". Repeat these steps for all remaining corners.

Figure 2

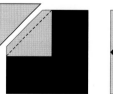

Make 9

Use your favorite technique to make half square triangles or use the following method.

Refer to Figure 3. Place fabric B and D $2^7/8$" squares right sides together. Cut them in half diagonally. Sew pairs of B and D triangles together on the wide edge. Press seam towards darker fabric and trim off dog ears.

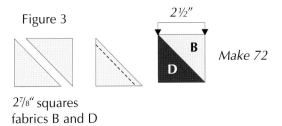

Figure 3

$2\frac{1}{2}$"

Make 72

$2^7/8$" squares
fabrics B and D

With right sides together, sew these half square triangles to fabric C and H $2^1/2$" squares as illustrated in Figure 4. Press seams as arrows indicate.

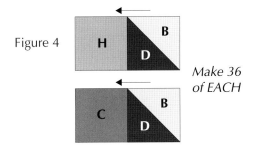

Figure 4

*Make 36
of EACH*

Sew these units together as illustrated in Figure 5. Press seam as arrow indicates.

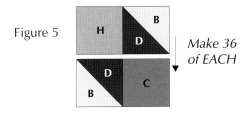

Figure 5

*Make 36
of EACH*

The next units are foundation pieced. Duplicate 36 foundations from the master foundations on page 122.

Refer to Figure 6 for fabric placement. Use fabric E $2^1/2$" squares, fabric F and G $3^1/4$" x $1^3/4$" rectangles and fabric C and D triangles to paperpiece units as illustrated. Paper can be removed when unit is finished.

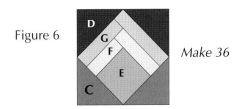

Figure 6

Make 36

Refer to Figure 7. Sew units together to form horizontal rows. Press seams as arrows indicate. To make Block A, sew rows together and press seams as arrows indicate.

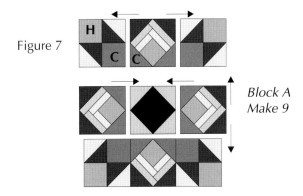

Figure 7

*Block A
Make 9*

Block B

Draw a diagonal line on the wrong side of fabric E and A $2^1/2$" squares.

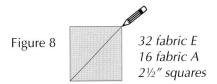

Figure 8

*32 fabric E
16 fabric A
$2\frac{1}{2}$" squares*

Refer to Figure 9. With right sides together, place fabric A $2^1/2$" squares on corners of fabric C $4^1/2$" squares. Stitch on the pencil line. Press seams towards outer edge and then trim seam allowance to measure $^1/4$". Repeat steps using fabric E $2^1/2$" squares and fabric B $4^1/2$" squares.

Figure 9

Make 4 *Make 16*

Refer to Figure 10. Sew units and fabric B 4$\frac{1}{2}$" squares together to form horizontal rows. Press seams as arrows indicate. To make Block B, sew rows together and press seams as arrows indicate.

Figure 10

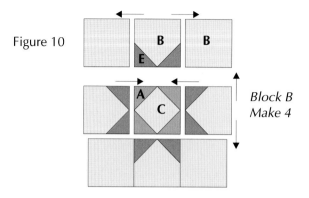

Block B
Make 4

Refer to Figure 11. Sew fabric B sashing and fabric J 2$\frac{1}{2}$" squares together. Press seams as arrows indicate.

Figure 11

Make 2

Make 2

Make 2

Refer to Figure 12. Sew sashing between blocks A and B as well as on each end of row as illustrated. Press seams as arrows indicate.

Figure 12

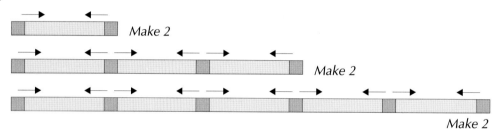

Make 2

Make 2

Make 1

Figure 13

To complete rows, sew units together as illustrated in Figure 13. Press seams as arrows indicate. Sew setting triangles and corner triangles to rows as illustrated and press.

Make 2

Make 2

Make 1

J

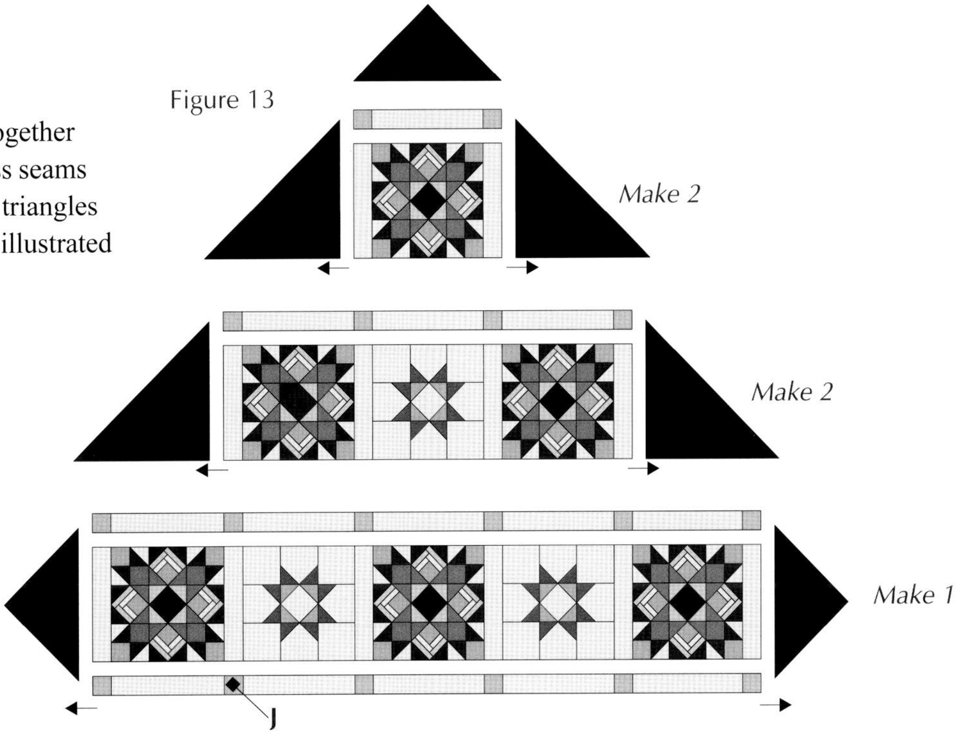

Refer to Figure 14. Sew rows together as illustrated. Press seams.

Figure 14

Borders

Measure the length of your quilt *(through the center of your quilt)* and piece 2 fabric D (1^1/2") inner border strips to that measurement. Sew to each side of the quilt and press towards outer edge. Apply inner border strips to top and bottom using the same technique.

Repeat these steps, this time using fabric A (5") strips for outer border.

Make 36 copies of foundations by using one of the following three methods.

1. Scan foundation into your computer and print out foundations.

2. Use a copying machine to make photocopies of foundations. You will get the best results if you make copies from the original rather than from a copy.

3. Trace foundation.

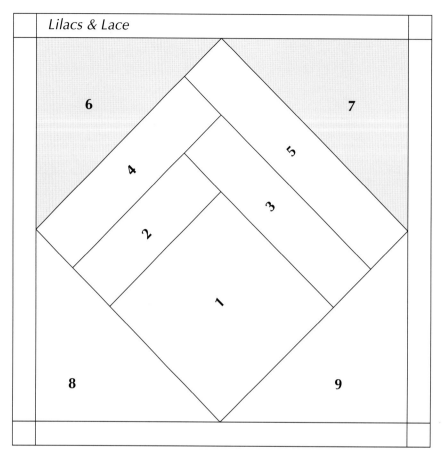

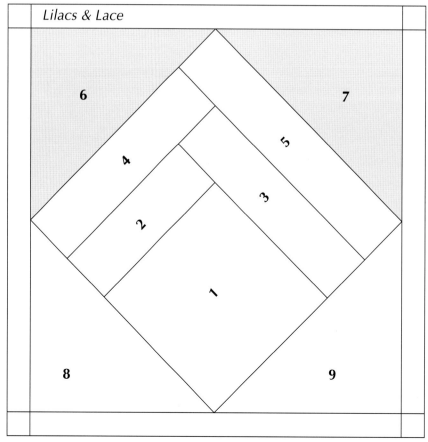

Midnight Sun *approximate size 74" x 74"*

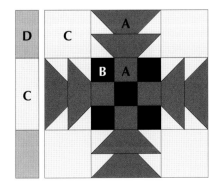

Fabric Requirements: *color photos are on pages 6 and 42*

Fabric A	$3\,^7/_8$* yards
Fabric B	$^1/_2$
Fabric C	$2^1/_2$
Fabric D	$2^3/_4$

Includes binding

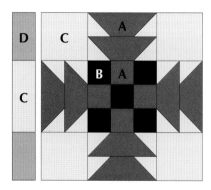

◣ *Do NOT cut these strips if you plan on making half square triangles by drawing a grid or using products such as Triangle Paper™ or Triangles on a Roll™*

Cutting Instructions for Midnight Sun

Fabric A

7 strips	$5^3/4$" wide	Cut into (104) $5^3/4$" x $2^1/4$" rectangles
6 strips	$2^1/4$" wide	Leave 4 strips whole
		Cut into (33) $2^1/4$" squares

Inner border 1 and outer border

16 strips	3" wide

Binding

8 strips	$2^1/2$" wide

Fabric B

5 strips	$2^1/4$" wide

Fabric C

6 strips	4" wide	Cut into (60) 4" squares
4 strips	$5^3/4$" wide	
13 strips	$2^1/4$" wide	Cut into (208) $2^1/4$" squares
◣ 2 strips	$2^5/8$" wide	Cut into (16) $2^5/8$" squares

Fabric D

◣ 2 strips	$2^5/8$" wide	Cut into (16) $2^5/8$" squares
7 strips	4" wide	

Setting triangles

1 strips	$12^1/2$" wide	Cut into (2) $12^1/2$" squares and *cut in half diagonally twice*
1 strip + scraps	11" wide	Cut into (8) 11" x $5^3/4$" rectangles

Corner triangles

1 strip	$13^1/4$" wide	Cut into (2) $13^1/4$" squares and *cut in half diagonally once*

Inner border 2

8 strips	$1^3/4$" wide

Freezer paper	Cut (8) $1^1/2$" x 10" rectangles

Sewing Instructions

Sew fabric A and B 2¹/4" strips right sides together lengthwise as illustrated in Figure 1. Press seams as arrows indicate. Cut pieced strip sets into 2¹/4" sections.

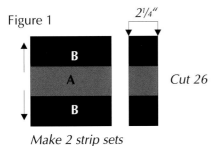

Figure 1

2¹/4"

Cut 26

Make 2 strip sets

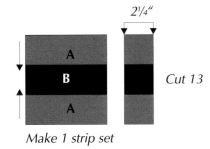

2¹/4"

Cut 13

Make 1 strip set

Sew these sections together in alternating order as illustrated in Figure 2. Press seams as arrows indicate.

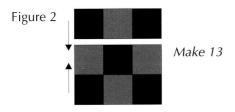

Figure 2

Make 13

Designer Tip: *To achieve a nicely joined seam intersection, nestle seams together before sewing. Do NOT place a pin at the intersecting point.*

Using a sharp pencil, draw a diagonal line on the wrong side of fabric C 2¹/4" squares. *(Using the Angler 2 or drawing a sewing guide onto your machine will eliminate this step.)*

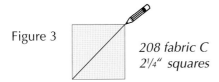

Figure 3

208 fabric C 2¹/4" squares

With right sides together, position fabric C 2¹/4" squares on the ends of fabric A 5³/4" x 2¹/4" rectangle as illustrated in Figure 4. Stitch on the pencil line. Press seams as arrows indicate and then trim seam allowance to measure ¹/4".

Figure 4

C

A

Make 104

Sew 2 of these units together as illustrated in Figure 5 and press seam as arrow indicates.

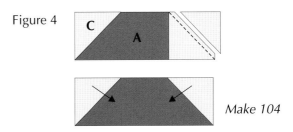

Figure 5

Make 52

Refer to Figure 6. Sew C/A units, A/B units and fabric C 4" squares into rows as illustrated. Press seams as arrows indicate. Refer to Designer Tip on page 126 for guidance on aligning diagonal seams to straight seams.

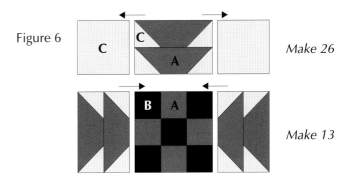

Figure 6

C

C

A

Make 26

B   A

Make 13

Designer Tip:

1. *On the wrong side of the fabric, draw a hatch mark on the diagonal seams $^1/4''$ from the edge of the fabric as shown in Figure 7. You will need to do this for units A/C.*

Figure 7

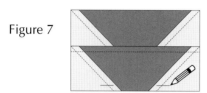

2. *With right sides together, align seams by positioning the straight seam so that it intersects the diagonal seam at the hatch mark. To insure precise alignment, insert a pin straight through the hatch mark and the other seam.*

3. *Complete the alignment by pinning to the right and left of the hatch mark. Remove alignment pin and sew pieces together.*

Make block by sewing rows together as illustrated in Figure 8. Press seams as arrows indicate.

Figure 8

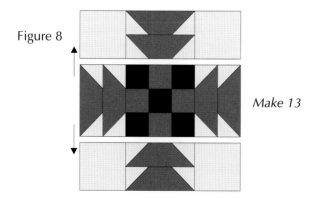

Make 13

Sew fabric C $5^3/4''$ and fabric D 4" strips together lengthwise as illustrated in Figure 9. Press seams as arrows indicate. Cut pieced strip sets into $2^1/4''$ sections. These units will be used for the sashing in Figure 16.

Figure 9

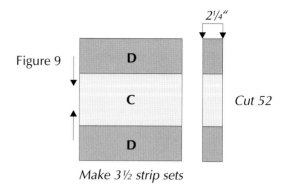

Cut 52

Make 3½ strip sets

Use your favorite technique to make half square triangles or use the following method.

Place fabric C and D $2^5/8''$ squares with right sides together. Cut them in half diagonally. Sew pairs of C and D triangles together on the wide edge. Press seam towards darker fabric and trim off dog ears.

Figure 10

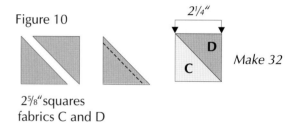

Make 32

$2^5/8''$ squares
fabrics C and D

Refer to Figure 11. Sew half square triangles together. Sew fabric A $2^1/4''$ squares to 8 of these units as illustrated. Press seams as arrows indicate.

Figure 11

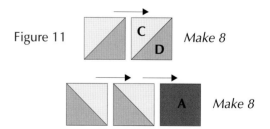

Make 8

Make 8

Sew these half square triangle units onto fabric C 4" square as illustrated in Figure 12. Press seams as arrows indicate.

Figure 12

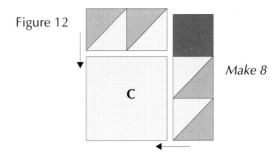

Make 8

Sew the unit you've just made onto end of fabric D 11" x 5³/4" rectangle as illustrated in Figure 13. Press seam as arrow indicate.

Figure 13

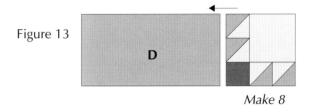

D

Make 8

Setting Triangles

Sew this unit to the short side of setting triangle as illustrated in Figure 14. Using a ruler and rotary cutter, trim off excess fabric so that triangle edge is even.

Figure 14

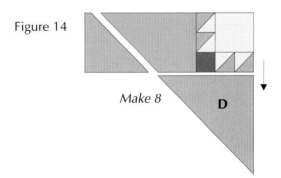

Make 8   D

Refer to Figure 15. Using a DRY iron, press shiny side of freezer paper onto WRONG side of pieced setting triangles.

Figure 15

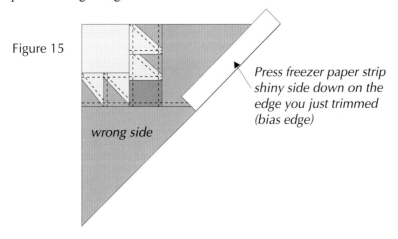

Press freezer paper strip shiny side down on the edge you just trimmed (bias edge)

wrong side

Refer to Figure 16. Sew C/D sashing and fabric A 2¹/₄" squares together as illustrated.

Refer to Figure 17. Sew sashing between blocks as well as on the end of each row as illustrated. Press seams as arrows indicate.

Figure 16

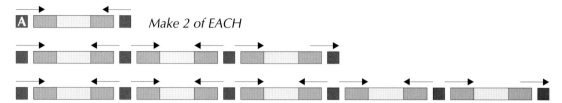

Make 2 of EACH

Figure 17

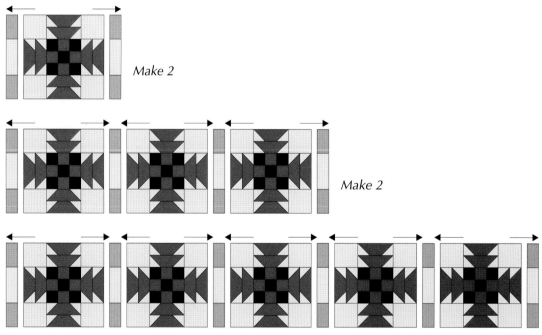

Make 2

Make 2

Make 1

To make rows, start by sewing pieced sashing and blocks together as illustrated in Figure 18. Press seams as arrows indicate. Add setting triangles and corner triangles. Sew rows together and press.

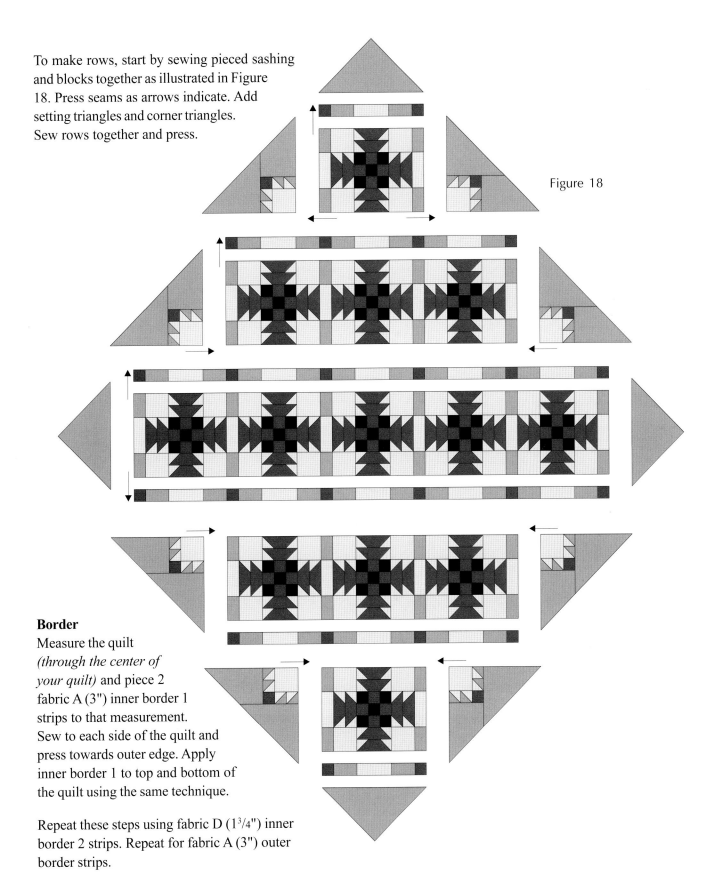

Figure 18

Border

Measure the quilt *(through the center of your quilt)* and piece 2 fabric A (3") inner border 1 strips to that measurement. Sew to each side of the quilt and press towards outer edge. Apply inner border 1 to top and bottom of the quilt using the same technique.

Repeat these steps using fabric D ($1^3/4$") inner border 2 strips. Repeat for fabric A (3") outer border strips.

Amsterdam Windmills *approximate size 74" x 74"*

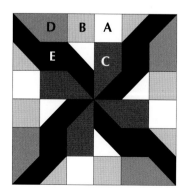

Fabric Requirements: *color photos are on pages 8 and 55*

Fabric A	1 yard
Fabric B	1
Fabric C	$1^1/8$
Fabric D	$1^1/3$
Fabric E	$4^3/4$*

*Includes binding

130

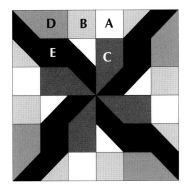

Cutting Instructions for Amsterdam Windmills

Fabric A

5 strips	2¹/2" wide	
6 strips	2¹/2" wide	Cut into (96) 2¹/2" squares

Fabric B

4 strips	2¹/2" wide	
6 strips	2¹/2" wide	Cut into (96) 2¹/2" squares

Fabric C

7 strips	4¹/2" wide

Fabric D

4 strips	4¹/2" wide

Inner Border

8 strips	2¹/2" wide

Fabric E

5 strips	6¹/2" wide	Cut into (80) 6¹/2" x 2¹/2" rectangles
3 strips	6¹/2" wide	Cut into (20) 6¹/2" x 4¹/2" rectangles
1 strip	4¹/2" wide	Cut into (16) 4¹/2" x 2¹/2" rectangle
13 strips	2¹/2" wide	Leave 2 strips whole
		Cut into (164) 2¹/2" squares

Outer border

8 strips	5¹/2" wide

Binding

8 strips	2¹/2" wide

Sewing Instructions

Refer to Figure 1. With right sides together, sew fabric C 4^1/$_2$" and fabric A 2^1/$_2$" strips together lengthwise. Press seam as arrow indicates. Cut pieced strip set into 2^1/$_2$" sections.

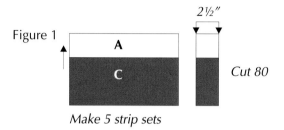

Make 5 strip sets

Repeat above steps, this time using fabric D 4^1/$_2$" and fabric B 2^1/$_2$" strips as illustrated in Figure 2.

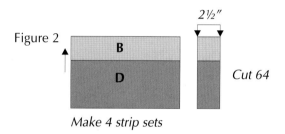

Make 4 strip sets

Repeat steps once again, this time using fabric C 4^1/$_2$" and fabric E 2^1/$_2$" strips as illustrated in Figure 3.

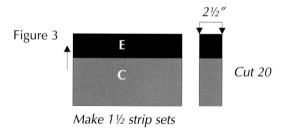

Make 1^1/$_2$ strip sets

Using a sharp pencil, draw a diagonal line on the wrong side of fabrics A, B and E 2^1/$_2$" squares. *(You can eliminate this step if you are using The Angler or have marked your sewing machine.)*

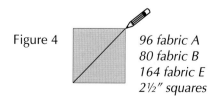

96 fabric A
80 fabric B
164 fabric E
2^1/$_2$" squares

With right sides together, position one fabric E 2^1/$_2$" square on each pieced A/C, B/D and E/C unit as illustrated in Figure 5. Stitch on the pencil line. Press seam allowance as arrows indicate and then trim to measure ^{1}/$_4$".

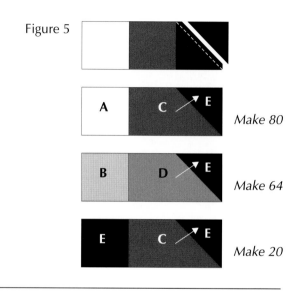

Make 80

Make 64

Make 20

NOTE: *Take a moment to double check that the diagonal seams of your units are oriented as in Figure 5. Likewise for Figure 6 below.*

With right sides together, position fabric A and B 2^1/$_2$" squares on fabric E 6^1/$_2$" x 2^1/$_2$" rectangle as illustrated in Figure 6. Sew on the pencil line. Press seam allowance as arrows indicate and then trim to measure ^{1}/$_4$".

Make 64

Position a fabric B 2^1/$_2$" square on fabric E 6^1/$_2$" x 4^1/$_2$" rectangle as illustrated in Figure 7. Sew on the pencil line. Press seam allowance as arrows indicate and then trim to measure ^{1}/$_4$".

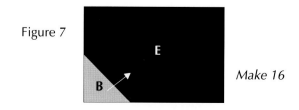

Make 16

Position fabric A 2^1/$_2$" square on fabric E 4^1/$_2$" x 2^1/$_2$" and 6^1/$_2$" x 2^1/$_2$" rectangles as illustrated in Figure 8. Sew on the pencil line. Press seam allowance as arrows indicate and then trim to measure ^{1}/$_4$".

Figure 8

Make 16 of each

Sew fabric B 2^1/$_2$" square to end of 4^1/$_2$" x 2^1/$_2$" E/A unit as illustrated in Figure 9. Press seam as arrow indicates.

Figure 9

Make 16

Arrange units together as illustrated in Figure 10. Before sewing, special care must be taken to align units with diagonal and straight seams. Refer to Designer Tip below for guidance on aligning diagonal seams to straight seams. Sew units together as illustrated in Figure 10. Press seams as arrows indicate.

Figure 10

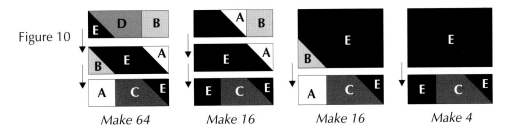

Make 64   *Make 16*   *Make 16*   *Make 4*

Designer Tip:

1. On the wrong side of the fabric, draw a hatch mark on the diagonal seam ^{1}/$_4$" from the edge of the fabric as shown in Figure 11. You will need to do this for units B/E/A, E/A and B/E.

Figure 11

2. With right sides together, align seams by positioning the straight seam so that it intersects the diagonal seam at the hatch mark. To insure precise alignment, insert a pin straight through the hatch mark and the other seam.

3. Complete the alignment by pinning to the right and left of the hatch mark. Remove alignment pin and sew pieces together.

Sew units together as illustrated in Figure 12 to form illustrated blocks. Undo several stitches in the seam allowance at the center of the block and press seams as arrows indicate. Do not skip this step — you'll be glad you have used this technique because all the converging seams will butt easily when you are sewing the blocks together.

Figure 12

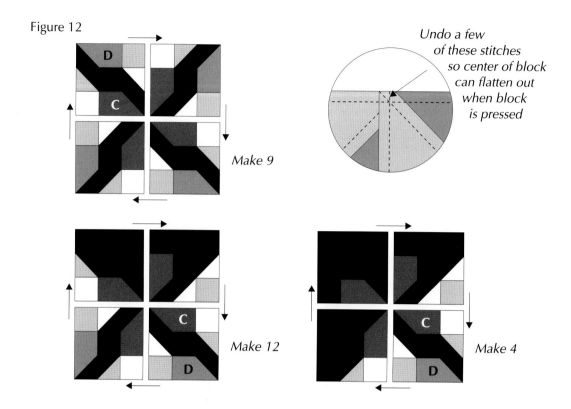

*Undo a few
of these stitches
so center of block
can flatten out
when block
is pressed*

Make 9

Make 12

Make 4

Figure 13

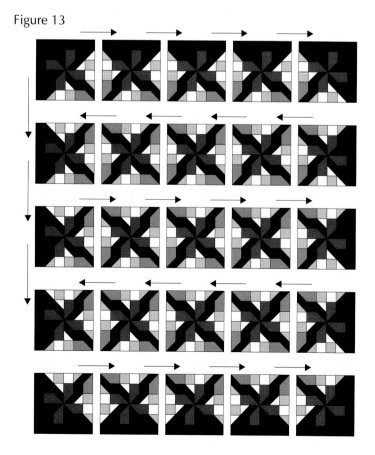

Sew blocks together as illustrated in Figure 13. Press seams as arrows indicate.

Border

Measure the length of your quilt *(through the center of the quilt)* and piece 2 fabric D (2¹/₂") inner border strips to that measurement. Sew to each side of the quilt and press seam towards outer edge. Apply inner borders to top and bottom using the same technique.

Apply fabric E (5¹/₂") outer borders using the same technique.

Oooh La La *approximate size 70" x 81"*

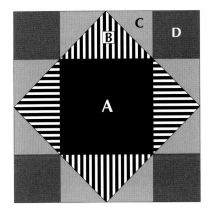

Fabric Requirements: *color photos are on pages 31 and 48*

Fabric A	3 1/2* yards
Fabric B	1 2/3
Fabric C	1 1/4
Fabric D	3/4
Fabric E	2 1/8

Includes binding

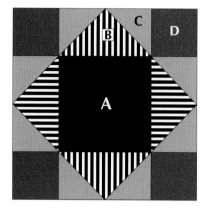

NOTE: *These cutting instructions are based on having 40" of usable fabric width. If your fabric is even slightly wider, you may have strips left over.*

Cutting Instructions for Oooh La La

Fabric A

4 strips	4½" wide	Cut into (30) 4½" squares
7 strips	2½" wide	Leave 5 strips whole
		Cut into (18) 2½" squares
3 strips	4" wide	Cut into (22) 4" squares

Outer border

8 strips	6½" wide

Binding

8 strips	2½" wide

Fabric B *stripes*

15 strips	2½" wide	Cut into (120) 2½" x 4½" rectangles

Inner Border

7 strips	1½" wide

Fabric C

15 strips	2½" wide	Cut into (240) 2½" squares

Fabric D

8 strips	2½" wide	Cut into (120) 2½" squares

Fabric E

3 strips	4½" wide	
3 strips	8½" wide	Cut into (20) 8½" x 4½" rectangles
4 strips	2½" wide	Cut into (18) 2½" x 8" rectangles

Setting triangles

2 strips	10" wide	Cut into (5) 10" squares and *cut in half diagonally twice*

Corner triangles

scraps	Cut into (2) 6¾" squares and *cut in half diagonally once*

Sewing Instructions

Using a sharp pencil, draw a diagonal line on the wrong side of 240 fabric C 2½" squares. *(Using the Angler 2 or drawing a sewing guide onto your machine will eliminate this step.)*

Figure 1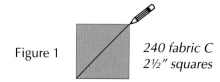

240 fabric C 2½" squares

Refer to Figure 2. With right sides together, position a fabric C 2^1/$_2$" square on one end of a fabric B 2^1/$_2$" x 4^1/$_2$" rectangle. Stitch on the pencil line. Press towards outer edge and then trim to measure ^{1}/$_4$". Repeat these steps for the other end.

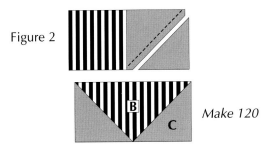

Figure 2

Make 120

Sew B/C units to fabric A 4^1/$_2$" square as illustrated in Figure 3. Press seams as arrows indicate.

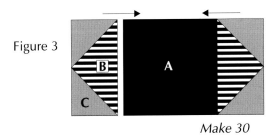

Figure 3

Make 30

Sew fabric D 2^1/$_2$" square to each end of remaining 60 B/C units as illustrated in Figure 4. Press seams as arrows indicate.

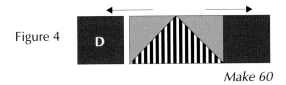

Figure 4

Make 60

Sew these units to long sides of A/B/C unit to form Block A as illustrated in Figure 5. Press seams as arrows indicate.

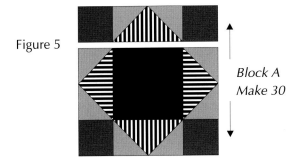

Figure 5

Block A
Make 30

Sew fabric E 4^1/$_2$" and A 2^1/$_2$" strips together lengthwise as indicated in Figure 6. Press seams as arrows indicate. Cut pieced strip sets into 2^1/$_2$" sections.

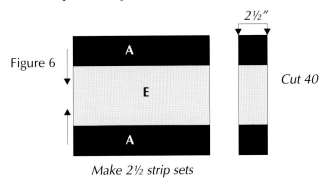

Figure 6

2½"

Cut 40

Make 2½ strip sets

Sew these fabric A/E units to fabric E 8^1/$_2$" x 4^1/$_2$" rectangles to form Block B as illustrated in Figure 7. Press seams as arrows indicate.

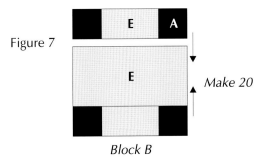

Figure 7

Make 20

Block B

Setting and Corner Triangles

Refer to Figure 8. Sew a fabric A 2^1/$_2$" square to one end of fabric E 2^1/$_2$" x 8" rectangle. Press seam as arrow indicates.

Figure 8

Make 18

Sew these units to short side of fabric E setting triangle as illustrated in Figure 9. Press seam as arrow indicates. Using a ruler and rotary cutter, trim off excess fabric so triangle edge is even.

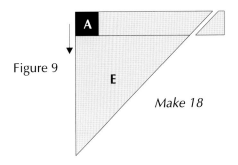

Figure 9

Make 18

Using a sharp pencil, draw a sewing line along the diagonal on the wrong side of fabric A 4" squares. *(Do this even if you usually don't draw pencil sewing lines.)*

Figure 10

22 fabric A
4" squares

Cut these squares in half along the other diagonal as illustrated in Figure 11. Notice that your cut is going across the pencil line.

Figure 11

Pencil line

With right sides together, align this fabric A triangle to the bottom corners of pieced setting triangles as illustrated in Figure 12. Stitch on the pencil line. Cut seam allowance to ¼" and carefully fingerpress as arrow indicates.

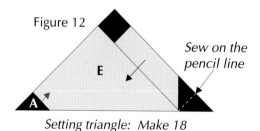

Figure 12

Sew on the
pencil line

E

A

Setting triangle: Make 18

Designer Tip: *Make sure that the angles of fabric A triangle are oriented exactly as illustrated in Figure 12 and Figure 13. Exercise care when handling and pressing setting and corner triangles so they do not get stretched out of shape.*

Refer to Figure 13. Align long side of fabric A triangle to long side of corner triangle *(the opposite of Figure 12)*. Stitch on the pencil line. Cut seam allowance to ¼" and carefully fingerpress as arrow indicates.

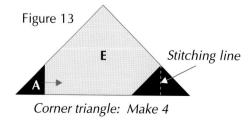

Figure 13

E

A

Stitching line

Corner triangle: Make 4

Sew blocks A, B, setting triangles and corner triangles together into rows as illustrated in Figure 14. Press seams as arrows indicate.

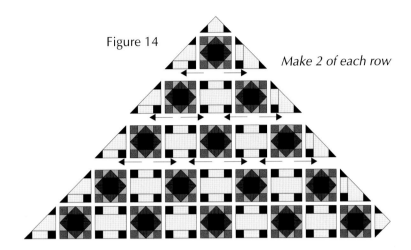

Figure 14

Make 2 of each row

Refer to Figure 15. Sew rows together to make quilt halves and press. Sew quilt halves together and press. If necessary, trim quilt edges so they are even.

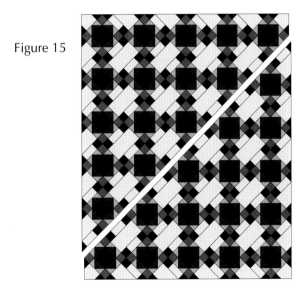

Figure 15

Border

Measure the length of the quilt *(through the center of the quilt)* and piece 2 fabric B inner border strips (1$^{1}/_{2}$") to that measurement. Sew to each side of the quilt and press towards outer edge. Apply inner border to top and bottom of the quilt using the same technique.

Repeat these steps, this time using fabric A (6$^{1}/_{2}$") strips for outer border.

■ NOTES ■

INDEX

ABOUT THE AUTHOR

Nicole Chambers is a quilt designer and quilting instructor known for her unique color sense and stylish quilt designs. Her clear, easy-to-follow instructions have been praised and appreciated by new and experienced quilters alike. In her last 2 books, *The Quilt Maniac's PLAYBOOK: Fuel for the Quilt Imagination and SIMPLE QUILTS that Look Like a Million Bucks*, many quilters learned the secrets of how to work with colors and fabric patterns to achieve the quilts they envision.

It became self evident very early in life that Nicole was born to be a quilter. She started building her stash at the tender age of 6 by charming all of the neighbor ladies into giving up their fabric scraps — much to the chagrin of her mother. Before starting her pattern company, *Nicole's Art to Live With* in 1994; Nicole used her creative design and writing skills by working for many years as a Communications Specialist for a variety of companies. Although she thoroughly enjoyed this career, when she found herself sneaking quilting books into the office in "plain brown wrappers," it was time to reconsider her career path. It was then that she decided to turn her talents towards the quilting world.

Nicole considers quilting to be a very important avenue of self expression and finds it no accident that so many women and men are such enthusiastic participants. It allows the creative spirit to soar while allowing us to leave a trail of memories behind to remind our loved ones just how dear they are.

She is committed to teaching and encouraging all quilters to honor their unique creativity, always coaxing them to stretch themselves a little with every quilting project. Motivated by the recognition that it can be hard to find time to indulge our passion to quilt as much as we would like to, Nicole writes her patterns with a keen eye towards quality. She remembers well the precious moments we finally have for ourself at the end of a taxing day, or the frustration we feel when we can't figure out what the next step is and at 2:00 AM find ourself wondering if it would be reasonable to ask the telephone operator if she quilts.

Nicole has won awards for both quilting and photography.

RESOURCES

Patterns and books are available at your local quilt shop or from
Tiger Lily Press
10013 SE Knight Street
Portland, OR 97266
(503) 788-6772
www.nicolechambers.com
www.quiltmaniac.com
tigerlilypress@msn.com

Other books and patterns by Nicole Chambers

Books:
- SIMPLE QUILTS that Look Like a Million Bucks

- The Quilt Maniac's PLAYBOOK: Fuel for the Quilt Imagination
    A Special Note to Quilt Teachers: *"The Ultimate Workshop Companion & Teachers Guide for The Quilt Maniac's PLAYBOOK" is now available to shop owners and quilt teachers. It features exclusive workshop sized versions of 9 queen sized quilts and has everything you need to give great workshops including handouts.*

Patterns:
- A Quilt for Betsy Ross
- Dancing in the Moonlight
- Smarter than the Average Bear
- Miss Eva's Garden
- Classroom Sampler
- Wild Roses from Milan
- Spring
- Summer
- Autumn
- Winter
- Apple Pie
- La Fleur

OOQ™ Mystery Series:
- Operation: Weather or Not
- The Rose Blooms at Midnight
- My Fine Feathered Friend
- A Night at the Opera
- The Moon Wore Sneakers

www.nicolechambers.com